HEATH
ALGEBRA 2
AN INTEGRATED APPROACH
LARSON, KANOLD, STIFF

TECHNOLOGY

USING CALCULATORS AND COMPUTERS

Neal Roys

Yvonne M. Coston

International Standard Book Number: 0-395-87203-0

1 2 3 4 5 6 7 8 9 10 HWI 01 00 99 98 97

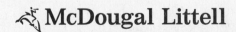

McDougal Littell

Evanston, Illinois • Boston • Dallas

Contents

Lesson

1.1	Introduction to Graphing Calculators	*1*
1.8	Constructing a Bar Graph	*4*
2.2	Guessing Equations of Lines	*6*
2.6	Guessing Absolute Value Equations	*9*
2.6	Graphs of Absolute Value Equations	*12*
2.7	Fitting a Line to Data	*14*
3.1	Solving a System of Linear Equations	*17*
4.4	Finding and Verifying Inverse Matrices	*19*
4.4	Writing a Cryptogram	*21*
4.6	Solving a System of Linear Equations	*23*
5.2	Guessing Quadratic Equations	*25*
5.2	Using the Zoom Features	*28*
5.3	Graphing Quadratic Equations	*31*
5.4	Evaluating the Quadratic Formula	*33*
6.2	Saving and Recalling Range Values	*35*
6.5	Transforming Graphs of Functions	*37*
6.7	Comparing Measures of Central Tendency	*40*
7.2	Guessing Exponential Equations	*42*
7.2	Exponential Decay and Half-Life	*45*
7.5	Solving a Radical Equation	*48*
8.5	Finding a Logarithmic Model	*50*
8.6	Solving Exponential Equations Graphically	*52*
9.2	Finding a Maximum Volume	*54*
9.3	Connecting Factors and Intercepts	*57*
9.4	Performing Synthetic Division	*59*
9.5	Finding Rational Zeros by Synthetic Division	*61*
9.6	Guessing Cubic Polynomials	*65*
9.7	Finding Measures of Dispersion	*68*
10.4	Solving Rational Equations	*71*
10.6	Constructing an Amortization Table	*73*
10.6	Finding Monthly Payments	*75*
11.2	Graphing Circles	*77*
11.3	Graphing Ellipses	*79*
11.5	Translating Conics	*81*
12.4	Finding the Sum of an Infinite Geometric Series	*83*
12.5	Finding Rows of Pascal's Triangle	*87*
12.6	Finding the Balance in an Annuity	*89*
13.2	Measuring Angles on the Unit Circle	*91*
13.3	Estimating Trigonometric Functions	*93*
14.1	Finding Amplitudes, Periods and Frequencies	*95*
14.2	Riding a Ferris Wheel	*97*
14.3	Sketching Conics with Parametric Equations	*99*
15.3	Using Combinations and Permutations	*101*
15.4	Experimenting with Probability	*103*
	Appendix A, TI-81 Keystrokes	*105*
	Appendix B, Casio FX-7700G Keystrokes	*106*
	Answers to Student Worksheets	*107*

Problem Solving Using a Graphing Calculator

This demonstration and worksheet can be used for group instruction or by individual students with graphing calculators. On their worksheets, students are asked to answer questions and complete exercises related to basic graphing calculator operations.

The objectives of this demonstration and worksheet are for students to be able to locate and use the following. **1.** The contrast keys **2.** The variable x and store keys **3.** The alphabet key **4.** The replay and cursor keys **5.** The insert and delete keys **6.** The negative and subtraction keys **7.** The exponent and absolute value keys **8.** The menus

1. THE CONTRAST KEYS

To make the screen darker or lighter, press the following keys. (The overhead projector may have a different method for contrast adjustment.)

TI-81: 2nd △ (hold) Darker   **CASIO fx-7700G**: MODE ▷ Darker

2nd ▽ (hold) Lighter   MODE ◁ Lighter

2. THE VARIABLE X AND STORE KEYS

Evaluate the expression $\frac{2}{3}x + 100$ when $x = 16.5$. (The value is 111.)

TI-81:   16.5 STO▷ X|T ENTER (2 ÷ 3) X|T + 100 ENTER

CASIO fx-7700G: 16.5 → X,θ,T EXE (2 ÷ 3) X,θ,T + 100 EXE

3. THE ALPHABET KEYS

The letters A through Z are located above the keys. Each letter of the alphabet can represent a variable in which a value can be stored. To see the value of the stored variable H, press ALPHA H ENTER or EXE. To store a value of 10 in H, press the following.

TI-81:   10 STO▷ H ENTER   **CASIO fx-7700G**:   10 → ALPHA H EXE

For many consecutive letters, you can activate the "Alpha-lock" key.

TI-81:   2nd A-LOCK A L G E B R A ⊔ ALPHA 1

CASIO fx-7700G: SHIFT A-LOCK A L G E B R A SPACE ALPHA 1

Press CLEAR or AC to clear the screen.

4. THE REPLAY AND CURSOR KEYS

Use to avoid retyping.

Suppose you need to evaluate the volume of two cylinders using the formula $V = \pi r^2 h$. Both have a radius of 17.8. The height of the first is 20 and the height of the second is 30. Instead of retyping the second calculation, you can use the replay and cursor keys.

TI-81:   2nd π × 17.8 x^2 × 20 ENTER △, Cursor to 2, Type 3, ENTER

CASIO fx-7700G:

SHIFT π × 17.8 SHIFT x^2 × 20 EXE ◁, Cursor to 2, Type 3, EXE

Use to make a correction.

Suppose you entered a formula incorrectly and need to make a change. You entered 33.4(11.2 + 15.7) when you meant to enter 33.7(11.2 + 15.7). To correct your error, use the replay and cursor keys.

TI-81:   33.4 $\boxed{(}$ 11.2 $\boxed{+}$ 15.7 $\boxed{)}$ $\boxed{\text{ENTER}}$ $\boxed{\triangle}$, Cursor to 4, Type 7, $\boxed{\text{ENTER}}$

CASIO fx-7700G: 33.4 $\boxed{(}$ 11.2 $\boxed{+}$ 15.7 $\boxed{)}$ $\boxed{\text{EXE}}$ $\boxed{\triangleleft}$, Cursor to 4, Type 7, $\boxed{\text{EXE}}$

5. THE INSERT AND DELETE KEYS

Suppose you entered 35.17(1.2 + 2.5) when you meant to enter 35.1(1.2 + 2.5). To correct your error, use the replay, cursor, and delete keys.

TI-81:   35.17 $\boxed{(}$ 1.2 $\boxed{+}$ 2.5 $\boxed{)}$ $\boxed{\text{ENTER}}$ $\boxed{\triangle}$, Cursor to 7, $\boxed{\text{DEL}}$ $\boxed{\text{ENTER}}$

CASIO fx-7700G: 35.17 $\boxed{(}$ 1.2 $\boxed{+}$ 2.5 $\boxed{)}$ $\boxed{\text{EXE}}$ $\boxed{\triangleleft}$, Cursor to 7, $\boxed{\text{DEL}}$ $\boxed{\text{EXE}}$

Suppose you entered 35.4(1.2 + 2.5) when you meant to enter 35.14(1.2 + 2.5). To correct your error, use the replay, cursor, and insert keys.

TI-81:   35.4 $\boxed{(}$ 1.2 $\boxed{+}$ 2.5 $\boxed{)}$ $\boxed{\text{ENTER}}$ $\boxed{\triangle}$, Cursor to 4, $\boxed{\text{INS}}$ 1 $\boxed{\text{ENTER}}$

CASIO fx-7700G: 35.4 $\boxed{(}$ 1.2 $\boxed{+}$ 2.5 $\boxed{)}$ $\boxed{\text{EXE}}$ $\boxed{\triangleleft}$, Cursor to 4, $\boxed{\text{SHIFT}}$ $\boxed{\text{INS}}$ 1 $\boxed{\text{EXE}}$

6. THE NEGATIVE AND SUBTRACTION KEYS

The negative key is $\boxed{(-)}$ and the subtraction key is $\boxed{-}$. To enter -8 − π or 50 − -1, use the following.

TI-81: $\boxed{(-)}$ 8 $\boxed{-}$ $\boxed{\text{2nd}}$ $\boxed{\pi}$ $\boxed{\text{ENTER}}$ **CASIO fx-7700G:** $\boxed{\text{SHIFT}}$ $\boxed{(-)}$ 8 $\boxed{-}$ $\boxed{\text{SHIFT}}$ $\boxed{\pi}$ $\boxed{\text{EXE}}$

50 $\boxed{-}$ $\boxed{(-)}$ 1 $\boxed{\text{ENTER}}$ 50 $\boxed{-}$ $\boxed{\text{SHIFT}}$ $\boxed{(-)}$ 1 $\boxed{\text{EXE}}$

7. THE EXPONENT AND ABSOLUTE VALUE KEYS

Some common powers such as x^2, x^3, $x^{1/2} = \sqrt{x}$, and $x^{1/3} = \sqrt[3]{x}$ have special keys. For other powers, such as 1.4^4, use the following.

TI-81:   1.4 $\boxed{\wedge}$ 4 $\boxed{\text{ENTER}}$ **CASIO fx-7700G:**   1.4 $\boxed{x^y}$ 4 $\boxed{\text{EXE}}$

To evaluate the absolute value of a number such as |2 − 4|, enter the following.

TI-81: $\boxed{\text{2nd}}$ $\boxed{\text{ABS}}$ $\boxed{(}$ 2 $\boxed{-}$ 4 $\boxed{)}$ $\boxed{\text{ENTER}}$

CASIO fx-7700G: $\boxed{\text{SHIFT}}$ $\boxed{\text{MATH}}$ $\boxed{\text{F3}}$ $\boxed{\text{F1}}$ $\boxed{(}$ 2 $\boxed{-}$ 4 $\boxed{)}$ $\boxed{\text{EXE}}$

8. THE MENUS

Many graphing calculator commands are on keys that activate menus. Activate the menus on the following keys and explore them using the four arrow keys.

TI-81: $\boxed{\text{MATH}}$, $\boxed{\text{2nd}}$ $\boxed{\text{TEST}}$, $\boxed{\text{PRGM}}$, $\boxed{\text{MATRX}}$, $\boxed{\text{2nd}}$ $\boxed{\text{STAT}}$,

$\boxed{\text{VARS}}$, $\boxed{\text{2nd}}$ $\boxed{\text{Y-VARS}}$, $\boxed{\text{ZOOM}}$

CASIO fx-7700G: $\boxed{\text{SHIFT}}$ $\boxed{\text{MATH}}$, $\boxed{\text{F1}}$, $\boxed{\text{PRE}}$ $\boxed{\text{F2}}$, $\boxed{\text{PRE}}$ $\boxed{\text{F3}}$,

$\boxed{\text{PRE}}$ $\boxed{\text{F4}}$, $\boxed{\text{PRE}}$ $\boxed{\text{SHIFT}}$ $\boxed{\text{PRGM}}$ $\boxed{\text{F1}}$, $\boxed{\text{PRE}}$ $\boxed{\text{F2}}$, $\boxed{\text{PRE}}$

Introduction to Graphing Calculators

Name _____

Problem Solving Using a Graphing Calculator

A graphing calculator is actually a hand-held computer. This set of exercises gives you an introduction to some of the basic features that make graphing calculators more powerful than non-graphing calculators.

EXERCISES

1. List the keystrokes for adjusting the contrast level on a graphing calculator. How do you make the screen darker? How do you make it lighter?

2. List two ways to enter the variable X on a graphing calculator.

3. List the keystrokes for storing the following values. Then store the values.
   a. 8 in the variable X **b.** 21 in the variable A **c.** -6 in the variable E
   d. 100 in the variable I **e.** π in the variable O **f.** 1.1^2 in the variable U

4. Use a graphing calculator to evaluate $216.9x - \frac{7}{8}x + \frac{4}{7}$ when $x = 8$.

5. Find the value of each variable in your first and last names. (Answers will vary.)

6. Type in your first and last names with a plus sign between them. Press ENTER or EXE. What does the answer mean?

7. Which key is the "replay" key on the graphing calculator you are using?

8. Press the replay key to cause your name to reappear. Use the cursor key to move the cursor to the plus sign. Type over the plus sign with a minus sign. Press ENTER or EXE. What does the answer mean?

9. Press the replay key. Delete the minus sign and your last name. Insert a plus sign between consecutive letters of your first name. Press ENTER or EXE. What does the answer mean?

10. Evaluate the following.
    a. 2^5 **b.** $\pi 4^2 (20)$ **c.** $17.3(3.4 + 5.2)$
    d. $12.2(6.12 - 5.67)$ **e.** $\dfrac{54.2 + 7.2}{11.3}$ **f.** $3.1\left(\dfrac{8.4 - 3.4 \cdot 1.4}{1.6}\right)$

11. Evaluate $\frac{9}{5}C + 32$ for $C = 39$.

12. Evaluate $\frac{5}{9}(F - 32)$ for $F = 70$.

*Problem Solving Using
a Graphing Calculator*

(See Exercises 8 and 9 on
page 54 of the text.)

This demonstration and worksheet can be used for group instruction or by individual students with graphing calculators. On their worksheets, students are asked to construct a bar graph and make conclusions based on the graph.

Before distributing the worksheet, you should go over the following example with your class.

EXAMPLE   CONSTRUCTING A BAR GRAPH

Use a graphing calculator to construct a bar graph and determine the mean for the following data. The data represents the number of hits that 17 players on a baseball team earned halfway through a season.

3, 5, 0, 2, 4, 0, 1, 3, 7, 4, 4, 3, 6, 3, 7, 6, 2

SOLUTION

Begin by setting the range, as shown at the right. x represents the number of hits and y represents the frequency. Next, enter the data.

RANGE
Xmin=0
Xmax=8
Xscl=1
Ymin=0
Ymax=5
Yscl=1

TI-81

2nd STAT ◁ 2 ENTER
2nd STAT ◁ 1
Enter data, pressing ENTER twice after each entry.
2nd QUIT

CASIO fx-7700G

SHIFT Defm 8 EXE AC
SHIFT CLR F2 EXE
MODE SHIFT 1 MODE ×
F2 F3 F1 SHIFT F5 EXE
Enter data in increasing order pressing F1 after each entry.

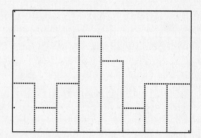

Finally, activate the graphing feature of the calculator.

TI-81:   2nd STAT ▷ 1 ENTER

CASIO fx-7700G: Graph EXE

You should obtain the graph shown at the right.

To determine the mean (or average) number of hits that the 17 players earned, you can use the following keystrokes.

TI-81:   2nd STAT 1 ENTER

CASIO fx-7700G: AC F4 F1 EXE

You should obtain a mean of 3.53.

Note: The *TI-81* and *Casio fx-7700G* will not produce graphs correctly unless they are set to the proper modes. If you are unsure of the correct modes, consult your calculator's user guide. Also, for the *TI-81*, clear the Y= screen.

*Problem Solving Using
a Graphing Calculator*

A graphing calculator can be used to construct a bar graph for data. On this worksheet, you are asked to construct a bar graph and then to make conclusions about the data. Once you have mastered the use of the calculator's bar-graphing capabilities, you should try using it to complete some of the exercises in the text. For instance, you could use a graphing calculator to work Exercise 9 on page 54.

EXERCISES

In Exercises 1–5, use the following information.

Twelve students were asked to write the total number of pieces of fruit that they normally eat in a week. The results were as follows.

4, 1, 0, 3, 3, 8, 4, 5, 4, 7, 5, 7

1. Let x represent the number of pieces of fruit and let y represent the frequency. Which of the following graphing calculator ranges is most appropriate for constructing a bar graph of the data.

a.
```
RANGE
Xmin=0
Xmax=10
Xscl=1
Ymin=0
Ymax=20
Yscl=1
```

b.
```
RANGE
Xmin=-8
Xmax=8
Xscl=1
Ymin=-8
Ymax=8
Yscl=1
```

c.
```
RANGE
Xmin=-8
Xmax=8
Xscl=1
Ymin=0
Ymax=8
Yscl=1
```

d.
```
RANGE
Xmin=0
Xmax=8
Xscl=1
Ymin=0
Ymax=4
Yscl=1
```

2. Construct a bar graph for the data. Then copy the results in the box that represents a blank screen at the right. (Use the range setting that you chose in Exercise 1.)

3. What is the average number of pieces of fruit eaten in a week by the twelve students?

4. Suppose that when recording the data, an error was made. One of the students that was listed as eating 4 pieces of fruit a week actually eats 7. Revise your bar graph to show the corrected data. Then copy the results in the box that represents a blank screen at the right.

5. What is the average number of pieces of fruit for the corrected data?

Exploration Using a Graphing Calculator

Program **GUESSLIN** is a game that can be played in a group instruction setting or on individual student graphing calculators. In either setting, the students should use the accompanying worksheet. (To save programming time, you may want to give the program to the students 1 or 2 days before you plan to use the activity in class.)

On their worksheets, students are asked to guess the values of the y-intercept and the slope of a line. When the program is executed, it randomly assigns values to m and b. The slope m is a multiple of 0.5 such that $-3 \leq m \leq 3$, and the y-intercept b is an integer such that $-5 \leq b \leq 5$. The program then displays the graph of $y = mx + b$. Note that after each guess, the program displays the original graph and the graph that corresponds to the guessed values of m and b.

TI-81 PROGRAM

```
Prgm8:GUESSLIN          :Disp "GUESS NUMBER"     :If (B=I)(M=R)=1
:IPart 11Rand−5→I       :Disp G                  :Goto 2
:0.5(IPart 13Rand−6)→R  :Disp "Y-INTERCEPT"      :G+1→G
:"I+RX"→Y₁              :Input B                  :Goto 1
:1→G                    :Disp "SLOPE"            :Lbl 2
:Lbl 1                  :Input M                  :Disp "CORRECT! YOU MADE"
:" "→Y₂                 :"B+MX"→Y₂               :Disp G
:DispGraph              :DispGraph               :Disp "GUESSES."
:Pause                  :Pause
```

CASIO fx-7700G PROGRAM

```
GUESSLINE               G◢                       Goto 1
Int(11Ran#−5)→I         "Y-INTERCEPT"            Lbl 2
0.5Int(13Ran#−6)→R      ?→B                      M=R⇒ Goto 3
1→G                     "SLOPE"                  G+1→G
Lbl 1                   ?→M                      Goto 1
Cls                     Graph Y=B+MX◢            Lbl 3
Graph Y=I+RX◢           B=I⇒Goto 2               "CORRECT! NUMBER OF GUESSES IS"
"GUESS NUMBER"          G+1→G                    G◢
```

Students can use this guessing program before they study Lesson 2.3 in the text. By doing this, you allow your students to discover the **slope-intercept** form of the equation of a line.

Before running the program, set the range as shown at the right. Also, for the *TI-81*, clear the Y= screen, and set the grid mode to **Grid On**.

```
RANGE
Xmin=-9
Xmax=9
Xscl=1
Ymin=-6
Ymax=6
Yscl=1
```

Here is a sample game using the **GUESSLIN** program. The student guessed the correct slope in 4 tries. The correct values for this game are $b = 4$ and $m = -2$. Notice that the first and last displays contain only one line.

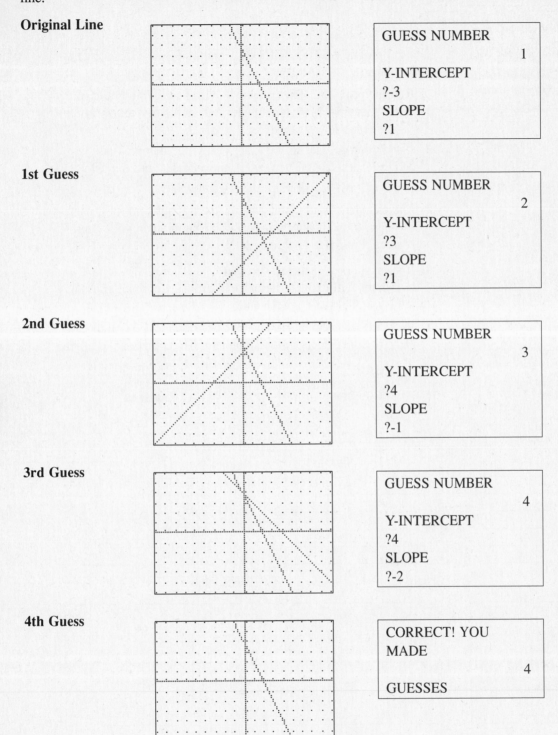

Original Line

GUESS NUMBER
             1

Y-INTERCEPT
?-3
SLOPE
?1

1st Guess

GUESS NUMBER
             2

Y-INTERCEPT
?3
SLOPE
?1

2nd Guess

GUESS NUMBER
             3

Y-INTERCEPT
?4
SLOPE
?-1

3rd Guess

GUESS NUMBER
             4

Y-INTERCEPT
?4
SLOPE
?-2

4th Guess

CORRECT! YOU MADE
             4
GUESSES

2.2

Name _____

Exploration Using a Graphing Calculator

Use the program **GUESSLIN** on a graphing calculator to complete each game.

1. Run the program. The calculator will display the graph of a line. Your goal is to use the graph to guess the values of the *y*-intercept and the slope.

2. Write your guesses in the spaces provided below. Press ENTER or EXE. Then enter your guesses into the calculator, pressing ENTER or EXE after each value.

3. The calculator will display the original graph and the graph of your guess. If both graphs are the same, then your guess is correct. Press ENTER or EXE.

4. If your guess is incorrect, press ENTER or EXE. The calculator will display the original graph. Continue guessing until you find the correct values.

5. Sketch the correct graph and write the correct equation. Describe the effects of the slope and *y*-intercept of the graph.

GAME 1			GAME 2			GAME 3	
Guesses			**Guesses**			**Guesses**	
B	M		B	M		B	M
1. _____ _____			1. _____ _____			1. _____ _____	
2. _____ _____			2. _____ _____			2. _____ _____	
3. _____ _____			3. _____ _____			3. _____ _____	
4. _____ _____			4. _____ _____			4. _____ _____	
5. _____ _____			5. _____ _____			5. _____ _____	
6. _____ _____			6. _____ _____			6. _____ _____	
7. _____ _____			7. _____ _____			7. _____ _____	
8. _____ _____			8. _____ _____			8. _____ _____	

Graph: **Graph:**   **Graph:**

Equation: _____   **Equation:** _____   **Equation:** _____

Patterns:

_____

_____

Guessing Absolute Value Equations

2.6

Exploration Using a Graphing Calculator

(See Exercises 9–14 on page 104 of the text.)

Program **GUESS.AV** is a game that can be played in a group-instruction setting or on individual student graphing calculators. In either setting, the students should use the accompanying worksheet. (To save programming time, you may want to give the program to the students 1 or 2 days before you plan to use the activity in class.)

On their worksheets, students are asked to guess the values of A, B, and C in the equation $y = A|x + B| + C$. When the program is run, it randomly assigns values to the three constants: A, B, and C are integers such that $-5 \leq A \leq 5$, $-5 \leq B \leq 5$ and $-5 \leq C \leq 5$. The program then displays the graph of $y = A|x + B| + C$. Students are asked to guess the values of A, B, and C. Note that after each guess, the program displays the original graph and the graph that corresponds to the "guessed" values of A, B, and C.

TI-81 PROGRAM

```
Prgm1:GUESS.AV
:0→G
:IPart 11Rand−5→A
:IPart 11Rand−5→B
:IPart 11Rand−5→C
:"A*abs(X+B)+C"→Y₁
:Lbl 1
:""→Y₂
:DispGraph

:G+1→G
:Pause
:ClrHome
:Disp "A*abs(X+B)+C"
:Disp "A="
:Input D
:Disp "B="
:Input E
:Disp "C="

:Input F
:"D*abs(X+E)+F"→Y₂
:DispGraph
:Pause
:If (A=D)(B=E)(C=F)≠1
:Goto 1
:Disp "YOU DID IT!"
:Disp "TOTAL GUESSES IS"
:Disp G
```

CASIO fx-7700G PROGRAM

```
GUESSAV
0→G
Int(11×Ran#)−5→A
Int(11×Ran#)−5→B
Int(11×Ran#)−5→C
Lbl 1
G+1→G
Cls
Graph Y=A×Abs(X+B)+C◢
"A×Abs(X+B)+C"

"A="
?→D
"B="
?→E
"C="
?→F
Graph Y=D×Abs(X+E)+F◢
0→X
0→Y

0→Z
A=D⇒1→X
B=E⇒1→Y
C=F⇒1→Z
XYZ→W
W≠1⇒Goto 1
"YOU DID IT!"
"TOTAL GUESSES IS"
G◢
```

Students can use this guessing program before they study Lesson 2.6 in the text. By doing this, you allow your students to discover relationships between the absolute-value equations and their graphs.

Before running the program, set the range as shown at the right. Also, on the *TI-81*, clear the Y= screen, and set the grid mode to **Grid On**.

RANGE
Xmin=-9
Xmax=9
Xscl=1
Ymin=-6
Ymax=6
Yscl=1

Here is a sample game using the **GUESS.AV** program. The student guessed the correct equation in 4 tries. The correct values for this game are $A = 2$, $B = -1$, and $C = -3$ Notice that the first and last displays contain only one graph.

Original Graph

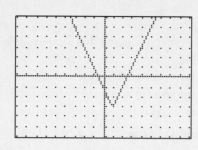

```
A*abs(X+B)+C
A=
?-1
B=
?1
C=
?2
```

1st Guess

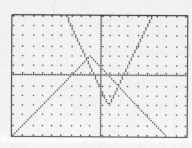

```
A*abs(X+B)+C
A=
?1
B=
?1
C=
?-2
```

2nd Guess

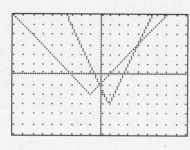

```
A*abs(X+B)+C
A=
?2
B=
?1
C=
?-3
```

3rd Guess

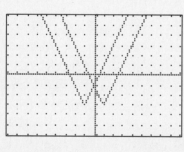

```
A*abs(X+B)+C
A=
?2
B=
?-1
C=
?-3
```

4th Guess

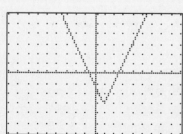

```
YOU DID IT!
TOTAL GUESSES
IS
                    4
```

Guessing Absolute Value Equations

Exploration Using a Graphing Calculator

Use the program **GUESS.AV** on a graphing calculator to complete each game.

1. Run the program. The calculator will display the graph of an equation $y = A|x + B| + C$. Your goal is to use the graph to guess the values of A, B, and C. A, B, and C are integers between -5 and 5.

2. Write your guesses in the spaces provided below. Press ENTER or EXE. Then enter your guesses into the calculator, pressing ENTER or EXE after each value.

3. The calculator will display the original graph and the graph of your guess. If both graphs are the same, then your guess is correct. Press ENTER or EXE.

4. If your guess is incorrect, press ENTER or EXE. The calculator will display the original graph. Continue guessing until you find the correct values.

5. Sketch the correct graph, and write the correct equation. Then describe the effects of A, B, and C on the graph.

GAME 1		
Guesses		
A	B	C
1. ___	___	___
2. ___	___	___
3. ___	___	___
4. ___	___	___
5. ___	___	___
6. ___	___	___
7. ___	___	___
8. ___	___	___

Graph:

Equation: _____

Patterns:

GAME 2		
Guesses		
A	B	C
1. ___	___	___
2. ___	___	___
3. ___	___	___
4. ___	___	___
5. ___	___	___
6. ___	___	___
7. ___	___	___
8. ___	___	___

Graph:

Equation: _____

GAME 3		
Guesses		
A	B	C
1. ___	___	___
2. ___	___	___
3. ___	___	___
4. ___	___	___
5. ___	___	___
6. ___	___	___
7. ___	___	___
8. ___	___	___

Graph:

Equation: _____

2.6

Exploration Using a
Graphing Calculator

(See Exercises 9–14 on
page 104 of the text.)

This demonstration and worksheet can be used for group instruction
or by individual students with graphing calculators.

The objective of this demonstration is for students to learn how to
graph an absolute value equation of the form $y = a|bx + c| + d$ on
a graphing calculator and use it to describe how the graph relates to
the graph of $y = |x|$.

EXAMPLE   DESCRIBING ABSOLUTE VALUE GRAPHS

Sketch the graphs of the following equations.

a. $y = |x|$ **b.** $y = |x| + 4$

c. $y = -|x|$ **d.** $y = |x - 7|$

Describe the relationship between the graph of $y = |x|$ and each of the
other three graphs.

SOLUTION

Begin by setting the range as shown at the right. Next, use the steps
shown on page 84 of the text to graph the four equations. You should
obtain the graph shown below.

RANGE
Xmin=-10
Xmax=10
Xscl=1
Ymin=-10
Ymax=10
Yscl=1

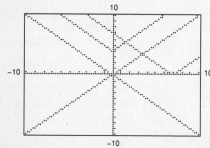

a. The graph of $y = |x|$ is $\vee$-shaped, opening upward with vertex at
(0, 0).

b. The graph of $y = -|x|$ is a reflection of the graph of $y = |x|$ in the
x-axis. The vertex is also at (0, 0).

c. The graph of $y = |x| + 4$ is the graph of $y = |x|$ shifted up 4 units. The
vertex is at (0, 4).

d. The graph of $y = |x - 7|$ is the graph of $y = |x|$ shifted 7 units to the
right. The vertex is at (7, 0).

Graphs of Absolute Value Equations

2.6

Name _____

Exploration Using a Graphing Calculator

On this worksheet, you are asked to use a graphing calculator to examine the graphs of absolute value equations of the form $y = a|bx + c| + d$.

EXERCISES

1. Describe how the graph of the given equation relates to the graph of $y = |x|$.

Given Equation	Horizontal Shift	Vertical Shift	Reflection
$y = -|x - 5| + 8$	_____	_____	_____
$y = |x| - 2$	_____	_____	_____
$y = |x - 5|$	_____	_____	_____
$y = -|x + 2| + 9$	_____	_____	_____
$y = 2|x + 3| - 4$	_____	_____	_____
$y = |\frac{1}{2}x + 6|$	_____	_____	_____

2. Find the vertex of each of the graphs in Exercise 1.

3. Sketch the graph of each equation in Exercise 1 by hand. Then use a graphing calculator to check your graphs. Copy your results in the spaces below.

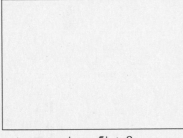

$y = -|x - 5| + 8$

$y = |x| - 2$

$y = |x - 5|$

$y = -|x + 2| + 9$

$y = 2|x + 3| - 4$

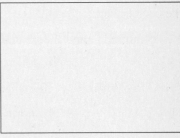

$y = |\frac{1}{2}x + 6|$

Problem Solving Using a Graphing Calculator

(See Exercises 13–18 on page 112 of the text.)

This demonstration and worksheet can be used for group instruction or by individual students with graphing calculators.

The objective of this activity is to prepare students for using a graphing calculator to find the best-fitting line for a collection of data. On their worksheets, students are asked to construct a scatter plot and determine the correlation coefficient for a collection of data by hand. Then they are asked to compare their results with the output from a graphing calculator.

EXAMPLE RECREATIONAL BOATS

For 1970 through 1989, the number of recreational boats, b (in millions), in the United States is shown in the table. Find an equation of the line that best fits this data. Then graph the line and the scatter plot for the data. (*Source: National Marine Manufacturers Association*)

Year	1970	1975	1980	1984	1985	1986	1987	1988	1989
Boats	8.8	9.7	11.8	13.5	13.8	14.3	14.5	15.1	15.6

SOLUTION

To begin, let $x = 0$ represent 1970. Clear all statistical data on your calculator. (For detailed steps, see Appendices A and B.) Enter the nine points into the graphing calculator. Use the range setting indicated at the right. Then, use the graphing calculator to find the equation of the best-fitting line.

TI-81: | 2nd | STAT | 2 | ENTER |

CASIO fx-7700G: | MODE | SHIFT | 3 | MODE | 4 | F6 | F1 | EXE | F2 | EXE | F3 | EXE |

For this data, you should obtain $a = 8.328514056$, $b = 0.3696787149$, and $r = 0.9934853888$. This implies that the equation of the best-fitting line is

$$y = 8.33 + 0.370x$$

and the correlation is $r = 0.993$.

```
RANGE
Xmin=0
Xmax=20
Xscl=2
Ymin=0
Ymax=20
Yscl=2
```

Now, graph this line and the scatter plot.

TI-81: | Y= | 8.33 | + | 0.370 | X|T | 2nd | STAT | ▷ | 2 | ENTER |

CASIO fx-7700G: | Graph | 8.33 | + | 0.370 | X,θ,T | EXE |

You should obtain the graph shown at the right.

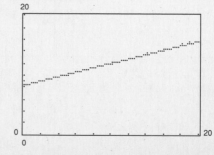

*Problem Solving Using
a Graphing Calculator*

On this worksheet, you are asked to find the best-fitting line and correlation coefficient for a collection of data by hand. Then you are asked to compare your results with results you obtain with a graphing calculator.

On a graphing calculator, the slope-intercept form of the equation of a line is displayed as $y = a + bx$ or $y = A + Bx$, where a (or A) is the y-intercept and b (or B) is the slope.

EXERCISES

1. Draw a scatter plot of the following data and sketch the line that appears to best fit the scatter plot.

   $(1, 1)$, $(2, 0.5)$, $(3, 5)$, $(4, 3)$, $(5, 4.5)$, $(6, 6)$, $(7, 9)$, $(8, 9)$, $(9, 7.5)$, $(10, 9)$

2. Choose two points that appear to be on the line and find the equation of the line that passes through the two points.

   $(x_1, y_1) =$ _____ $(x_2, y_2) =$ _____

   $m =$ _____   Equation: _____

3. Enter the data in a graphing calculator. Be sure to clear all statistical data before entering the data. Also, on the *TI-81*, clear the $\boxed{Y=}$ screen. Find the best-fitting line.

   TI-81: $\boxed{\text{2nd}}$ $\boxed{\text{STAT}}$ $\boxed{2}$ $\boxed{\text{ENTER}}$

   CASIO fx-7700G: $\boxed{\text{MODE}}$ $\boxed{\text{SHIFT}}$ $\boxed{3}$ $\boxed{\text{MODE}}$ $\boxed{4}$ $\boxed{\text{F6}}$ $\boxed{\text{F1}}$ $\boxed{\text{EXE}}$ $\boxed{\text{F2}}$ $\boxed{\text{EXE}}$ $\boxed{\text{F3}}$ $\boxed{\text{EXE}}$

   $a =$ _____ $b =$ _____

   $r =$ _____   Equation: _____

4. Graph the scatter plot of the data and the line that you obtained in Exercise 3 on the same screen. (Use the indicated range.) Then copy your result in the blank box below.

   RANGE
   Xmin=-1
   Xmax=11
   Xscl=1
   Ymin=0
   Ymax=10
   Yscl=1

5. Complete the table. (In the table, $\overline{x}$ is the average of the x-coordinates and $\overline{y}$ is the average of the y-coordinates.)

x_i	$x_i - \overline{x}$	$(x_i - \overline{x})^2$	y_i	$y_i - \overline{y}$	$(y_i - \overline{y})^2$	$(x_i - \overline{x})(y_i - \overline{y})$
1			1			
2			0.5			
3			5			
4			3			
5			4.5			
6			6			
7			9			
8			9			
9			7.5			
10			9			
Sum						

6. Calculate the correlation coefficient using the following formula.

$$r = \frac{\text{sum of } (x_i - \overline{x})(y_i - \overline{y})}{\sqrt{[\text{sum of } (x_i - \overline{x})^2][\text{sum of } (y_i - \overline{y})^2]}}$$

Compare your results to the value of r obtained in Exercise 3.

Solving a System of Linear Equations	3.1

Problem Solving Using a Graphing Calculator

(See Exercises 25–36 on page 126 of the text.)

This demonstration and worksheet can be used for group instruction or by individual students with graphing calculators. On their worksheets, students are asked to use a graphing calculator to solve a system of linear equations.

The objective of this demonstration and worksheet is for students to learn how to use a graphing calculator to find the coordinates of the point of intersection of two graphs. (This topic is also discussed in the Graphing Calculator feature found on page 128 of the text.)

To illustrate the technique, you can use the following example, which shows how to use a graphing calculator to solve the system in Example 3 on page 123 of the text.

EXAMPLE   FINDING THE SCORE ON AN EXAM

On a college entrance exam, you answered 80 of the 85 questions. Each correct answer adds 1 point to your raw score, each unanswered question adds nothing, and each incorrect answer subtracts $\frac{1}{4}$ point. Your raw score was 70. How many questions did you answer correctly?

SOLUTION

As shown on page 123 of the text, you can use a system of linear equations to solve this problem. Letting x be the number of correct answers and y be the number of incorrect answers, produces the following system.

$$\begin{cases} x + y = 80 & \text{Equation 1} \\ x - \frac{1}{4}y = 70 & \text{Equation 2} \end{cases}$$

To solve this system graphically, you first need to write each equation in slope-intercept form.

$$\begin{cases} y = -x + 80 & \text{Equation 1} \\ y = 4x - 280 & \text{Equation 2} \end{cases}$$

Before drawing the graph of this system, you should try to estimate a reasonable range (or viewing rectangle). From the nature of the problem you know that both x and y must be positive and less than or equal to 80. The graph for the indicated range is shown below at the left. After zooming in once (with a zoom factor of 4), you can use the trace feature to approximate the solution to be $x = 72$ and $y = 8$.

RANGE
Xmin=0
Xmax=80
Xscl=10
Ymin=0
Ymax=80
Yscl=10

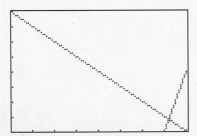

Graph with Original Range

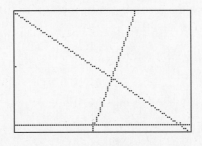

Graph after Zooming In Once

3.1

Name _____

*Problem Solving Using
a Graphing Calculator*

In Lesson 3.1 in the text, you learned how to solve a system of two linear equations by sketching the graph of each equation and locating the point of intersection of the two graphs.

Before entering each equation, you need to rewrite the equation in slope-intercept form. For instance, you should rewrite $2x + y = 4$ as $y = -2x + 4$, and you should rewrite $x - y = 7$ as $y = x - 7$.

When hunting for the point of intersection, you need to pay special attention to your choice of a range. If the point of intersection doesn't appear on the screen, you should keep changing the range until the point appears. After you find the point of intersection, you can zoom in (with a zoom factor of 4) to approximate the coordinates of the point to the desired accuracy.

EXERCISES

In Exercises 1–4, match the system of linear equations with the range that shows the solution of the system.

1. $\begin{cases} x - 2y = 4 \\ -2x + y = 7 \end{cases}$
2. $\begin{cases} x - y = 15 \\ 5x + 3y = 27 \end{cases}$
3. $\begin{cases} 2x + 3y = 2 \\ x + 6y = 10 \end{cases}$
4. $\begin{cases} \frac{1}{2}x + y = 8 \\ -x + 2y = 8 \end{cases}$

a.
```
RANGE
Xmin=5
Xmax=10
Xscl=1
Ymin=-10
Ymax=-5
Yscl=1
```

b.
```
RANGE
Xmin=2
Xmax=8
Xscl=1
Ymin=2
Ymax=8
Yscl=1
```

c.
```
RANGE
Xmin=-8
Xmax=0
Xscl=1
Ymin=-8
Ymax=0
Yscl=1
```

d.
```
RANGE
Xmin=-4
Xmax=2
Xscl=1
Ymin=-1
Ymax=4
Yscl=1
```

In Exercises 5–8, use a graphing calculator to solve the system of linear equations.

5. $\begin{cases} 2x + y = 10 \\ 3x - y = 10 \end{cases}$
6. $\begin{cases} 4x - y = -7 \\ -x + 2y = 7 \end{cases}$
7. $\begin{cases} 4x + 3y = 5 \\ 3x - 2y = 25 \end{cases}$
8. $\begin{cases} -x + 2y = -5 \\ 2x - y = 1 \end{cases}$

9. A total of $6000 is invested in two funds paying 5% and 8% annual interest. The combined annual interest is $336. Assign labels to the following verbal model. Then solve the resulting linear system to find how much of the $6000 is invested in each fund.

$$\boxed{\begin{array}{c}\text{Amount in}\\ \text{5\% fund}\end{array}} + \boxed{\begin{array}{c}\text{Amount in}\\ \text{8\% fund}\end{array}} = \boxed{\begin{array}{c}\text{Total}\\ \text{invested}\end{array}}$$

$$\boxed{5\%} \cdot \boxed{\begin{array}{c}\text{Amount in}\\ \text{5\% fund}\end{array}} + \boxed{8\%} \cdot \boxed{\begin{array}{c}\text{Amount in}\\ \text{8\% fund}\end{array}} = \boxed{\begin{array}{c}\text{Total}\\ \text{interest}\end{array}}$$

Exploration Using a Graphing Calculator

(See Exercises 7–16 and 27–34 on pages 200 and 201 of the text.)

This demonstration and worksheet can be used for group instruction or by individual students with graphing calculators. On their worksheets, students are asked to calculate determinants and use them to find the inverses of matrices. Then, they are asked to use a graphing calculator to verify their results.

The objective of this demonstration and worksheet is to help students understand how to use a graphing calculator to find and verify inverse matrices.

EXAMPLE   FINDING AND VERIFYING AN INVERSE MATRIX

Determine the inverse of the following matrix.

$$A = \begin{bmatrix} 3 & -1 \\ 4 & -6 \end{bmatrix}$$

Then verify your result by showing that

$$A \times A^{-1} = \begin{bmatrix} 1 & 0 \\ 0 & 1 \end{bmatrix} = A^{-1} \times A.$$

SOLUTION

Begin by setting your calculator to display all output with three significant digits.

TI-81:   [MODE], Cursor to 3, [ENTER] [2nd] [QUIT]

CASIO fx-7700G: [SHIFT] [DISP] [F1] 3 [EXE]

Next, enter matrix A into the calculator.

TI-81

[MATRX] [▷] [1] 2 [ENTER] 2 [ENTER]
Enter contents of matrix A,
pressing [ENTER] after each entry.
[2nd] [QUIT]

CASIO fx-7700G

[MODE] [0] [F1] [F6] [F1] 2 [EXE] 2 [EXE]
Enter contents of matrix A,
pressing [EXE] after each entry.
[PRE]

On the *CASIO fx-7700G* screen, the matrix will appear. To view the matrix on the *TI-81* screen, press [2nd] [[A]] [ENTER].

Next, find the inverse of A and store the result in B.

TI-81:   [2nd] [[A]] [x^{-1}] [ENTER] [STO▷] [2nd] [[B]] [ENTER]

CASIO fx-7700G: [F1] [F4] [F2]

You should obtain the matrix shown at the right. You can check the result by calculating $A \times B$ and $B \times A$.

$$B = \begin{bmatrix} 0.429 & -0.071 \\ 0.286 & -0.214 \end{bmatrix}$$

TI-81

$A \times B$:   [2nd] [[A]] [×] [2nd] [[B]] [ENTER]
$B \times A$:   [2nd] [[B]] [×] [2nd] [[A]] [ENTER]

CASIO fx-7700G

$A \times B$:   [PRE] [F5]
$B \times A$:   [PRE] [F1] [F5] [PRE] [F5]

(Note that on the *CASIO fx-7700G*, the contents of A and B are now switched.) Because $A \times B$ and $B \times A$ are both equal to the 2×2 identity matrix, you can conclude that A and B are inverses of each other.

Exploration Using a Graphing Calculator

On this worksheet, you are asked to calculate the determinant of a square matrix and use it to find the inverse of the matrix. Then you are asked to use a graphing calculator to verify your result.

To obtain the matrix product $A \times B$ on your graphing calculator, press the following keystrokes.

TI-81: ⎡2nd⎤ ⎡[A]⎤ ⎡×⎤ ⎡2nd⎤ ⎡[B]⎤ ⎡ENTER⎤

CASIO fx-7700G: ⎡PRE⎤ ⎡F5⎤

To obtain the matrix product $B \times A$ on your graphing calculator, press the following keystrokes.

TI-81: ⎡2nd⎤ ⎡[B]⎤ ⎡×⎤ ⎡2nd⎤ ⎡[A]⎤ ⎡ENTER⎤

CASIO fx-7700G: ⎡PRE⎤ ⎡F1⎤ ⎡F5⎤ ⎡PRE⎤ ⎡F5⎤

EXERCISES

1. The determinant of a 2×2 matrix $A = \begin{bmatrix} a & b \\ c & d \end{bmatrix}$ is $|A| = ad - bc$. Find the determinant of the following matrices.

    a. $A = \begin{bmatrix} 7 & -4 \\ -5 & 3 \end{bmatrix}$ **b.** $B = \begin{bmatrix} 5 & 2 \\ 2 & 1 \end{bmatrix}$ **c.** $C = \begin{bmatrix} 6 & -2 \\ 7 & -2 \end{bmatrix}$

2. Use a graphing calculator to find the determinants of the matrices in Exercise 1. After entering each matrix in A, press the following keystrokes.

    TI-81: ⎡MATRX⎤ ⎡5⎤ ⎡2nd⎤ ⎡[A]⎤ ⎡ENTER⎤

    CASIO fx-7700G: ⎡F3⎤

3. Try entering a "nonsquare" matrix into your graphing calculator. Then, try to evaluate the determinant of the matrix. What is the result? What can you conclude?

4. Use the fact that the inverse of $A = \begin{bmatrix} a & b \\ c & d \end{bmatrix}$ is

    $$A^{-1} = \frac{1}{|A|} \begin{bmatrix} d & -b \\ -c & a \end{bmatrix}$$

    to find the inverses of the matrices in Exercise 1.

5. Use a graphing calculator to verify the result of Exercise 4. (Show that $A \times A^{-1} = I = A^{-1} \times A$.)

    a. Enter the original matrix in A and the inverse matrix in B.

    b. Find the matrix products $A \times B$ and $B \times A$. If both products are equal to the 2×2 identity matrix, then A and B are inverses of each other.

6. Use a graphing calculator to find the inverse of each matrix in Exercise 1. After entering each matrix in A, press the following keystrokes.

    TI-81: ⎡2nd⎤ ⎡[A]⎤ ⎡x^{-1}⎤ ⎡ENTER⎤

    CASIO fx-7700G: ⎡F4⎤

Writing a Cryptogram

4.4

Problem Solving
Using a Computer

(See Exercises 35–38 on
page 201 of the text.)

This demonstration and worksheet can be used for group instruction or by individual students with computers that have BASIC. On their worksheets, students are asked to use a BASIC program to encode a message.

The objective of this demonstration and worksheet is to help students understand how computers can be used in cryptography.

BASIC PROGRAM

```
10  DIM MES$(350), UNC(350), COD(350)
20  DIM A(2,2)
30  READ X$
40  M = LEN(X$): L = (M MOD 2)
50  IF L=1 THEN M = M+1: X$ = X$ + " "
60  PRINT "MESSAGE: ";
70  FOR I=1 TO M
80      MES$(I) = MID$(X$,I,1)
90      PRINT MES$(I);
100 NEXT I: PRINT
110 PRINT "UNCODED MESSAGE: ";
120 FOR I=1 TO M
130     UNC(I) = ASC(MES$(I))−64
140     IF UNC(I)=-32 THEN UNC(I)=0
150     PRINT UNC(I);
160 NEXT I: PRINT
170 FOR I=1 TO 2
180     FOR J=1 TO 2
190         READ A(I,J)
200     NEXT J
210 NEXT I
220 PRINT "CODED MESSAGE: ";
230 FOR I=1 TO M−1  STEP  2
240     COD(I)=UNC(I)*A(1,1)+UNC(I+1)*A(2,1)
250     COD(I+1)=UNC(I)*A(1,2)+UNC(I+1)*A(2,2)
260     PRINT COD(I);COD(I+1);
270 NEXT I
280 END
360 DATA "STOP NOW"
370 DATA -1,2,2,-3
```

When this program is run, it will produce the following printout.

MESSAGE: STOP NOW
UNCODED MESSAGE: 19 20 15 16 0 14 15 23
CODED MESSAGE: 21 -22 17 -18 28 -42 31 -39

This message is the same as that given in Example 4 on page 198 of the text. To code a different message, change the data on line 360. To use an encoding matrix other than

$$A = \begin{bmatrix} -1 & 2 \\ 2 & -3 \end{bmatrix}$$

change the data on line 370.

*Problem Solving
Using a Computer*

On this worksheet, you are asked to use a BASIC program to encode a message.

EXERCISES

1. What is the uncoded message for the message WELL DONE?

2. Using the following encoding matrix, what is the coded message for the message WELL DONE?

$$\begin{bmatrix} -2 & -3 \\ 3 & 4 \end{bmatrix}$$

3. What changes must be made in the BASIC program to encode the message WELL DONE using the encoding matrix given in Exercise 2?

4. Run the BASIC program (with the changes made in Exercise 3). Write the output in the space below. What do you notice about the results?

MESSAGE: _____
UNCODED MESSAGE: _____
CODED MESSAGE: _____

In Exercises 5–8, use the BASIC program and the given matrix to encode the message.

5. $\begin{bmatrix} 5 & -7 \\ 3 & -4 \end{bmatrix}$, SEND MONEY

MESSAGE: _____
UNCODED MESSAGE: _____
CODED MESSAGE: _____

6. $\begin{bmatrix} 1 & -1 \\ -6 & 5 \end{bmatrix}$, HOME SWEET HOME

MESSAGE: _____
UNCODED MESSAGE: _____
CODED MESSAGE: _____

7. $\begin{bmatrix} 6 & 7 \\ -1 & -1 \end{bmatrix}$, OVER THE HILL

MESSAGE: _____
UNCODED MESSAGE: _____
CODED MESSAGE: _____

8. $\begin{bmatrix} 2 & -3 \\ -5 & 7 \end{bmatrix}$, ROSES ARE RED

MESSAGE: _____
UNCODED MESSAGE: _____
CODED MESSAGE: _____

Problem Solving Using a Graphing Calculator

(See Exercises 11–19 on page 213 of the text.)

This demonstration and worksheet can be used for group instruction or by individual students with graphing calculators. On their worksheets, students are asked to use the matrix capability of a graphing calculator to solve a system of linear equations.

The objective of this demonstration and worksheet is for students to learn how to create an augmented matrix to represent a system of linear equations. They are then asked to apply elementary row operations to solve the system.

When demonstrating the following example, point out that a major benefit of performing elementary row operations with technology is to lessen the opportunity to make a careless arithmetic error. (Note: The *Casio fx-7700G* performs matrix operations, but does not perform elementary row operations on a matrix.)

The elementary row operations that can be performed on the rows of an augmented matrix are as follows.

RowSwap([A],n,m)   *Interchange Row n and Row m.*

Row+([A],n,m)   *Add Row n to Row m.*

*Row(c,[A],n)   *Multiply Row n by c.*

*Row+(c,[A],n,m)   *Multiply Row n by c and add the result to Row m.*

EXAMPLE USING AN AUGMENTED MATRIX TO SOLVE A LINEAR SYSTEM

Use an augmented matrix to solve the system $\begin{cases} x + y = 1 \\ -x + 3y = -9 \end{cases}$.

SOLUTION

1. Begin by forming the augmented matrix $\begin{bmatrix} 1 & 1 & \vdots & 1 \\ -1 & 3 & \vdots & -9 \end{bmatrix}$.

2. Enter the matrix into the graphing calculator. (See the instructions on page 194 of the text.)

3. Perform elementary row operations on the matrix as follows.

TI-81	*Description*	*Resulting Matrix*
Row+([A],1,2)→[A]	Add Row 1 to Row 2.	$\begin{bmatrix} 1 & 1 & \vdots & 1 \\ 0 & 4 & \vdots & -8 \end{bmatrix}$
*Row(1/4,[A],2)→[A]	Multiply Row 2 by $\frac{1}{4}$.	$\begin{bmatrix} 1 & 1 & \vdots & 1 \\ 0 & 1 & \vdots & -2 \end{bmatrix}$
*Row+(-1,[A],2,1)→[A]	Add -1 times Row 2 to Row 1.	$\begin{bmatrix} 1 & 0 & \vdots & 3 \\ 0 & 1 & \vdots & -2 \end{bmatrix}$

4. Rewrite the augmented matrix as a system of linear equations.

$$\begin{cases} x = 3 \\ y = -2 \end{cases}$$

From the "reduced" system, the solution is evident.

4.6

Name _____

Problem Solving Using a Graphing Calculator

One way to solve a system of linear equations is to use an **augmented matrix**.

Linear System

$$\begin{cases} x + y = 1 \\ -x + 2y = -9 \end{cases}$$

Augmented Matrix

$$\begin{bmatrix} 1 & 1 & \vdots & 1 \\ -1 & 2 & \vdots & -9 \end{bmatrix}$$

Begin by entering the augmented matrix into your graphing calculator. Then use any of the following elementary row operations to solve the system.

RowSwap([A],n,m)   *Interchange Row n and Row m.*

Row+([A],n,m)   *Add Row n to Row m.*

*Row(c,[A],n)   *Multiply Row n by c.*

*Row+(c,[A],n,m)   *Multiply Row n by c and add the result to Row m.*

Your goal is to rewrite the augmented matrix in the form

$$\begin{bmatrix} 1 & 0 & \vdots & a \\ 0 & 1 & \vdots & b \end{bmatrix}.$$

From this augmented matrix, you can rewrite the linear system as

$$\begin{cases} x \quad = a \\ \quad y = b \end{cases}$$

to see that the solution is $x = a$ and $y = b$.

EXERCISES

1. Enter the matrix $\begin{bmatrix} 3 & 1 & \vdots & 7 \\ -3 & 2 & \vdots & -13 \end{bmatrix}$ as matrix A in your calculator.

   a. Add Row 1 to Row 2 and store the result as matrix A.   Row+([A],1,2)→[A]

   b. Multiply Row 2 by $\frac{1}{3}$ and store the result as matrix A.   *Row(1/3,[A],2)→[A]

   c. Add -1 times Row 2 to Row 1 and store the result as matrix A.   *Row+(-1,[A],2,1)→[A]

   d. Multiply Row 1 by $\frac{1}{3}$.   *Row(1/3,[A],1)→[A]

   What does the final matrix tell you about the solution of the system? Explain.

In Exercises 2–7, use an augmented matrix to solve the system of linear equations. Explain your steps.

2. $\begin{cases} 2x + 3y = 8 \\ 3x - 2y = -1 \end{cases}$

3. $\begin{cases} x + 5y = -9 \\ -2x + 7y = 1 \end{cases}$

4. $\begin{cases} 3x + 5y = -21 \\ -4x + 3y = -30 \end{cases}$

5. $\begin{cases} x + 4y - 2z = 16 \\ 2x + y + 4z = 1 \\ -x + 5y + 2z = -7 \end{cases}$

6. $\begin{cases} x + 3y + z = 16 \\ 2x - 2y + 4z = -4 \\ 3x - y + 6z = 4 \end{cases}$

7. $\begin{cases} 2x + 4y - z = 13 \\ x - y + 2z = -16 \\ -3x + y - 3z = 21 \end{cases}$

Guessing Quadratic Equations

5.2

Teacher Demonstration Material

Problem Solving Using a Graphing Calculator

Program **GUESSPAR** is a game that can be played in a group instruction setting or on individual student graphing calculators. In either setting, the students should use the accompanying worksheet. (To save programming time, you may want to give the program to the students 1 or 2 days before you plan to use the activity in class.)

On their worksheets, students are asked to guess the values of A, B, and C in the equation $y = A(x + B)^2 + C$. When the program is executed, it randomly assigns values to the constants A, B, and C: A, B, and C are integers such that $-5 \le A \le 5$, $-5 \le B \le 5$, and $-5 \le C \le 5$. The program then displays the graph of $y = A(x + B)^2 + C$. Note that after each guess, the program displays the original graph and the graph that corresponds to the guessed values of A, B, and C.

TI-81 PROGRAM

```
Prgm1:GUESSPAR
:Ipart 11Rand−5→A
:Ipart 11Rand−5→B
:Ipart 11Rand−5→C
:"A(X+B)²+C"→Y₁
:1→G
:Lbl 1
:ClrHome
:""→Y₂
:DispGraph
:Pause
:Disp "GUESS NUMBER"
:Disp G
:Disp "A(X+B)²+C"
:Disp "A="
:Input D
:Disp "B="
:Input E
:Disp "C="
:Input F
:"D(X+E)²+F"→Y₂
:DispGraph
:Pause
:If (A=D)(B=E)(C=F)=1
:Goto 2
:G+1→G
:Goto 1
:Lbl 2
:Disp "CORRECT! NUMBER"
:Disp "OF GUESSES IS"
:Disp G
```

CASIO fx-7700G PROGRAM

```
GUESSPAR
Int 11Ran#−5→A
Int 11Ran#−5→B
Int 11Ran#−5→C
1→G
Lbl 1
Cls
Graph y=A(X+B)²+C◢
"GUESS NUMBER"
G◢
"A="
?→D
"B="
?→E
"C="
?→F
Graph=D(X+E)²+F◢
0→X
0→Y
0→Z
A=D⇒1→X
B=E⇒1→Y
C=F⇒1→Z
XYZ→W
W=1⇒Goto 2
G+1→G
Goto 1
Lbl 2
"CORRECT! NUMBER"
"OF GUESSES IS"
G◢
```

This game is designed to allow students to discover the effect of the constants A, B, and C on the graph of $y = A(x + B)^2 + C$.

Before running the program, set the range as shown at the right. Also, on the *TI-81*, clear the [Y=] screen, and set the grid mode to **Grid On**.

RANGE
Xmin=-9
Xmax=9
Xscl=1
Ymin=-6
Ymax=6
Yscl=1

Here is a sample game using the **GUESSPAR** program. The student guessed the correct values in 4 tries. The correct values for this game are $A = -3$, $B = 3$ and $C = 1$. Notice that the first and last displays contain only one graph.

Original Graph

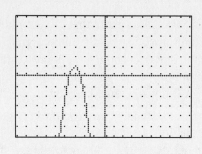

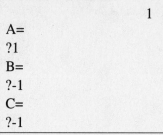

GUESS NUMBER

1

A=
?1
B=
?-1
C=
?-1

1st Guess

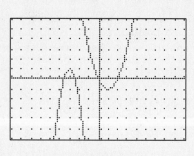

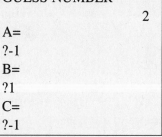

GUESS NUMBER

2

A=
?-1
B=
?1
C=
?-1

2nd Guess

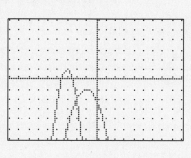

GUESS NUMBER

3

A=
?-3
B=
?2
C=
?1

3rd Guess

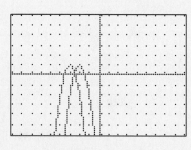

GUESS NUMBER

4

A=
?-3
B=
?3
C=
?1

4th Guess

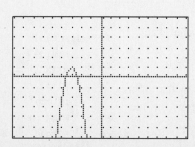

CORRECT! NUMBER
OF GUESSES IS

4

Exploration Using a
Graphing Calculator

Use the program **GUESSPAR** on a graphing calculator to complete each game.

1. Run the program. It will display the graph of an equation $y = A(x + B)^2 + C$. Your goal is use the graph to guess the values of A, B, and C. A, B, and C are integers between -5 and 5.

2. Write your guesses in the spaces provided below. Press ENTER or EXE. Then enter your guesses into the calculator, pressing ENTER or EXE after each value.

3. The calculator will display the original graph and the graph of your guess. If both graphs are the same, then your guess is correct. Press ENTER or EXE.

4. If your guess is incorrect, press ENTER or EXE. The calculator will display the original graph. Continue guessing until you find the correct values.

5. Sketch the correct graph, and write the correct equation. Then describe the effects of A, B, and C on the graph.

GAME 1

Guesses

A B C

1. ___ ___ ___
2. ___ ___ ___
3. ___ ___ ___
4. ___ ___ ___
5. ___ ___ ___
6. ___ ___ ___
7. ___ ___ ___
8. ___ ___ ___

Graph:

Equation: _____

Patterns:

GAME 2

Guesses

A B C

1. ___ ___ ___
2. ___ ___ ___
3. ___ ___ ___
4. ___ ___ ___
5. ___ ___ ___
6. ___ ___ ___
7. ___ ___ ___
8. ___ ___ ___

Graph:

Equation: _____

GAME 3

Guesses

A B C

1. ___ ___ ___
2. ___ ___ ___
3. ___ ___ ___
4. ___ ___ ___
5. ___ ___ ___
6. ___ ___ ___
7. ___ ___ ___
8. ___ ___ ___

Graph:

Equation: _____

Using the Zoom Features

5.2

Problem Solving Using a Graphing Calculator

This demonstration and worksheet can be used for group instruction or by individual students with graphing calculators.

The objective of this demonstration and worksheet is for students to learn how to use the zoom features of a graphing calculator.

EXAMPLE 1 PATH OF A SHOT PUT

The path of Natalya Lisovskaya's winning 1988 Olympic shot put can be modeled by $y = -0.01464x^2 + x + 5$. Graph this equation on a graphing calculator.

SOLUTION

Begin by setting the range as indicated at the right. Next, graph the equation. (Use the steps shown on page 84 of the text.) You should obtain the graph shown below at the left. Because the entire path is not shown, you can zoom out (with a zoom factor of 4).

TI-81: ZOOM 3 ENTER

CASIO fx-7700G: F2 F4

```
RANGE
Xmin=-10
Xmax=10
Xscl=1
Ymin=-10
Ymax=10
Yscl=1
```

Continue zooming out until the entire path is shown.

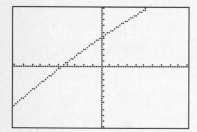

Graph with Original Range

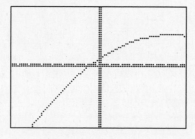

After Zooming Out Once

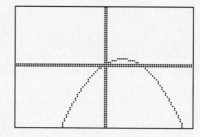

After Zooming Out Twice

Because Natalya's shot put path is represented by the portion of the curve that lies above the x-axis, you can obtain a better view by using the zoom box.

TI-81: ZOOM 1, cursor to upper left corner at about (-10, 35), ENTER, cursor to lower right corner at about (80, -10), ENTER

CASIO fx-7700G: F2 F1, cursor to upper left corner at about (-10, 35), EXE, cursor to lower right corner at about (80, -10), EXE

You should obtain the graph shown below at the right.

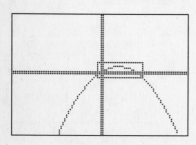

Set Zoom Box

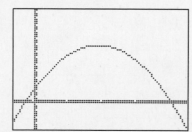

After Using Zoom Box

EXAMPLE 2   COMPARING SHOT PUT PATHS

In Example 2, the equation represents the path of a shot put thrown at
45°. The equations of the paths of shot puts thrown at 40° and 50° are
as follows.

$$40° :\ y = -0.0125x^2 + 0.84x + 5$$

$$50° :\ y = -0.0177x^2 + 1.19x + 5$$

Which of the three shot puts traveled the farthest?

SOLUTION

Use the range setting indicated below.

> **RANGE**
> Xmin=-10
> Xmax=80
> Xscl=1
> Ymin=-10
> Ymax=35
> Yscl=1

Next, graph all three equations (the two shown above and the one from
Example 1) on the same screen. From the screen, you cannot tell which
shot put went the farthest. Use the zoom box feature until you obtain a
graph that shows which throw went the farthest.

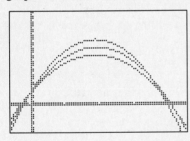   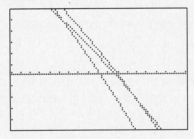   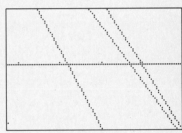

Graph with Original Range   After Using Zoom Box Once   After Using Zoom Box Twice

From the screen shown above at the right, you can conclude that the 45°
throw went the farthest.

*Problem Solving Using
a Graphing Calculator*

On this worksheet, you are asked to use the zoom out and zoom box
features of a graphing calculator.

EXERCISES

1. From 1950 through 1990, the average annual consumption, C, of cigarettes
   per American (18 or older) can be modeled by

   $$C = 4025.5 + 51.4x - 3.1x^2$$

   where $x = 0$ corresponds to 1960. Set your range as indicated at the right
   and use the zoom box feature to obtain a good view of the graph. Copy
   the results in the blank screen below.

   ```
   RANGE
   Xmin=-10
   Xmax=30
   Xscl=1
   Ymin=0
   Ymax=10000
   Yscl=1
   ```

In Exercises 2–5, use the following information.

The paths of the water from a sprinkler for three different settings are
given below.

$$35° : y = -0.06x^2 + 0.70x + 0.5$$
$$60° : y = -0.16x^2 + 1.73x + 0.5$$
$$75° : y = -0.60x^2 + 3.73x + 0.5$$

2. Use the range setting shown at the right to graph all three equations on the
   same screen. Use the zoom box feature to obtain a view so that all three
   graphs fit well on the screen. Copy the result in the blank screen below.

   ```
   RANGE
   Xmin=-20
   Xmax=20
   Xscl=1
   Ymin=-10
   Ymax=10
   Yscl=1
   ```

3. Which angle sends water the farthest?

4. Which angle sends water the highest?

5. Which angle sends water the shortest distance?

6. Use the range setting shown at the right to graph $y = |40 - 15x| + 15$.
   Use the zoom box feature to obtain a view so that the graph fits well on
   the screen. Copy the result in the blank screen below.

   ```
   RANGE
   Xmin=-10
   Xmax=10
   Xscl=1
   Ymin=-10
   Ymax=10
   Yscl=1
   ```

Screen for Exercise 1   Screen for Exercise 2   Screen for Exercise 6

*Exploration Using a
Graphing Calculator*

This demonstration and worksheet can be used for group instruction or by individual students with graphing calculators. On their worksheets, students are asked to use a graphing calculator to solve a system of linear equations.

The objective of this demonstration and worksheet is for students to learn how to graph a quadratic equation of the form

$$y = a(bx + c)^2 + d$$

on a graphing calculator, *and* learn how the graph relates to the graph of $y = x^2$.

EXAMPLE   DESCRIBING GRAPHS OF QUADRATIC EQUATIONS

Sketch the graphs of the following equations.

   a. $y = x^2$ **b.** $y = (x - 3)^2$

   c. $y = (x - 3)^2 + 4$ **d.** $y = \text{-}(x - 3)^2$

Describe the relationship between the graph of $y = x^2$ and each of the other graphs.

RANGE
Xmin=-10
Xmax=10
Xscl=1
Ymin=-10
Ymax=10
Yscl=1

SOLUTION

Begin by setting the range as shown at the right. Next, graph $y = x^2$. You should obtain the graph shown below at the left. Notice that the graph is a parabola opening upward with a vertex at (0, 0). Now, graph the remaining equations on the same screen. You should obtain the graph shown below at the right.

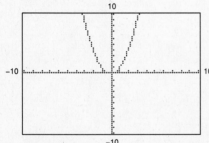
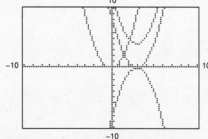

b. The graph of $y = (x - 3)^2$ is the graph of $y = x^2$ shifted three units to the right. The parabola opens upward and its vertex is at (3, 0).

c. The graph of $y = (x - 3)^2 + 4$ is the graph of $y = x^2$ shifted three units to the right and four units up. The parabola opens upward and its vertex is at (3, 4).

d. The graph of $y = \text{-}(x - 3)^2$ is the graph of $y = x^2$ reflected in the x-axis and shifted three units to the right. The parabola opens downward and its vertex is at (3, 0).

5.3

Name _____

On this worksheet, you are asked to use a graphing calculator
to examine the graphs of quadratic equations of the form
$y = a(bx + c)^2 + d$.

EXERCISES

1. Describe how the graph of the given equation relates to the graph of $y = x^2$.

Given Equation	Horizontal Shift	Vertical Shift	Reflection
$y = x^2 - 2$	_____	_____	_____
$y = (x - 6)^2$	_____	_____	_____
$y = (x + 1)^2 - 3$	_____	_____	_____
$y = -(x - 2)^2 - 4$	_____	_____	_____
$y = -(x + 5)^2 + 8$	_____	_____	_____
$y = (x + 4)^2 + 3$	_____	_____	_____

2. Find the vertex of each of the graphs in Exercise 1.

3. Sketch the graph of each equation in Exercise 1 by hand. Then use a
graphing calculator to check your results. Copy the results in the blank
screens below.

$y = x^2 - 2$	$y = (x - 6)^2$	$y = (x + 1)^2 - 3$

$y = -(x - 2)^2 - 4$	$y = -(x + 5)^2 + 8$	$y = (x + 4)^2 + 3$

Problem Solving Using a Graphing Calculator

(See Exercises 21–30 on page 255 of the text.)

This demonstration and worksheet can be used for group instruction or by individual students with graphing calculators. On their worksheets, students are asked to evaluate the quadratic formula using the editing and replay features of a graphing calculator.

The objective of this demonstration and worksheet is for students to understand when parentheses must be used in the quadratic formula.

EXAMPLE   SOLVING A VERTICAL MOTION MODEL

According to the vertical motion model, an object with an initial height of 125 feet and an initial velocity of 80 feet per second has a height, H (in feet), given by

$$H = 125 + 80t - 16t^2$$

where t is the time in seconds. Find the times at which the object has a height of zero.

SOLUTION

The solutions of a quadratic equation of the form $y = ax^2 + bx + c$ are

$$x = \frac{-b \pm \sqrt{b^2 - 4ac}}{2a}. \qquad \text{\textit{Quadratic Formula}}$$

By setting H equal to 0, you can find the times at which the object has a height of zero by solving the equation $0 = 125 + 80t - 16t^2$. The solutions are given by the quadratic formula, as follows.

$$t = \frac{-80 + \sqrt{80^2 - 4(-16)(125)}}{2(-16)} \quad \text{and} \quad t = \frac{-80 - \sqrt{80^2 - 4(-16)(125)}}{2(-16)}$$

To evaluate the first solution, you can use the following keystrokes.

TI-81: $\boxed{(}$ $\boxed{(-)}$ 80 $\boxed{+}$ $\boxed{\text{2nd}}$ $\boxed{\sqrt{}}$ $\boxed{(}$ 80 $\boxed{x^2}$ $\boxed{-}$ 4 $\boxed{\times}$ $\boxed{(-)}$ 16 $\boxed{\times}$ 125 $\boxed{)}$ $\boxed{)}$
$\boxed{\div}$ $\boxed{(}$ 2 $\boxed{\times}$ $\boxed{(-)}$ 16 $\boxed{)}$ $\boxed{\text{ENTER}}$

CASIO fx-7700G: $\boxed{(}$ $\boxed{\text{SHIFT}}$ $\boxed{(-)}$ 80 $\boxed{+}$ $\boxed{\sqrt{}}$ $\boxed{(}$ 80 $\boxed{\text{SHIFT}}$ $\boxed{x^2}$ $\boxed{-}$ 4 $\boxed{\times}$ $\boxed{\text{SHIFT}}$ $\boxed{(-)}$ 16 $\boxed{\times}$ 125 $\boxed{)}$ $\boxed{)}$
$\boxed{\div}$ $\boxed{(}$ 2 $\boxed{\times}$ $\boxed{\text{SHIFT}}$ $\boxed{(-)}$ 16 $\boxed{)}$ $\boxed{\text{EXE}}$

Your calculator should display -1.25. To obtain the other solution, activate the replay feature and change the expression as follows.

TI-81: $\boxed{\triangle}$, cursor to +, $\boxed{-}$ $\boxed{\text{ENTER}}$

CASIO fx-7700G: $\boxed{\triangleleft}$, cursor to +, $\boxed{-}$ $\boxed{\text{EXE}}$

You should obtain 6.25. Because a negative time does not make sense in this problem, you can conclude that the only solution is 6.25 seconds.

*Problem Solving Using
a Graphing Calculator*

On this worksheet, you are asked to use a graphing calculator to evaluate the quadratic formula. The replay and editing features of a graphing calculator can make evaluation of the quadratic formula more efficient.

EXERCISES

1. The initial velocity of an object is 90 feet per second. Its initial height is 15 feet above the ground. Use the vertical motion model

   $$H = -16t^2 + vt + s$$

   to write the model for the height of this object.

2. To find the time at which the object in Exercise 1 is at ground level, let $H = 0$. When the resulting quadratic equation is written in standard form, what are the values of a, b, and c?

3. Use the quadratic formula to write the solutions of the equation in Exercise 2. Then use a graphing calculator to evaluate the solution involving "+" (rather than "−").

4. Use the replay and edit features of the graphing calculator to evaluate the other value of t without retyping the expression.

5. Do both of the solutions obtained in Exercises 3 and 4 make sense? Explain.

6. Which of the following is the correct way to enter the quadratic formula to find one of the values of t for $-16t^2 - 20t + 180$?

   a. $20+\sqrt{((-20)^2-4*-16*180)/-32}$
   b. $(20+\sqrt{(-20^2-4*-16*180))/-32}$
   c. $(20+\sqrt{(-20)^2-4*-16*180)/-32}$
   d. $(20+\sqrt{((-20)^2-4*-16*180))/-32}$

7. The following keystrokes were entered to evaluate the quadratic formula. Each, however, is incorrect. Correct the mistake in each. Then evaluate the expression correctly.

   a. $(-620+\sqrt{620^2-4*14*180})/28$ (*Display*: -360)
   b. $-20+\sqrt{(20^2-4*-16*100)}/(2*-16)$ (*Display*: -22.57694102)
   c. $(45+\sqrt{(-45^2-4*-16*208)})/-32$ (*Display*: -4.726259177)

8. Suppose you accidentally forgot to enclose the discriminant in parentheses in the expression $(13+\sqrt{13^2-4*1*5})/2$. On which symbol would you place the cursor to insert the left parenthesis? On which symbol would you place the cursor to insert the right parenthesis?

Problem Solving Using a Graphing Calculator

This demonstration and worksheet can be used for group instruction or by individual students with graphing calculators. On their worksheets, students are asked to find solutions of equations.

The objective of this demonstration and worksheet is for students to estimate solutions of equations using the following six-step graphing calculator procedure.

1. Find the range values such that each solution is visible on the screen.
2. Save the range values using the program **RANGESAV**.
3. Zoom in to estimate a solution to the nearest hundredth.
4. Recall the saved range values using the program **RECALRNG**.
5. Review the graph.
6. Repeat steps 3–5 until all solutions are found.

TI-81 Program   (*The CASIO fx-7700G does not permit this type of program.*)

PrgmA: RANGESAV		PrgmB: RECALRNG	
:Xmin→A	Ymin→D	A→Xmin	D→Ymin
:Xmax→B	Ymax→E	B→Xmax	E→Ymax
:Xscl→C	Yscl→F	C→Xscl	F→Yscl

EXAMPLE   FINDING SOLUTIONS OF AN EQUATION

Find all solutions of $|2x - 48| - 1.652 = 0$, accurate to 0.01.

SOLUTION

Begin by entering the programs listed above. Then graph the equation $y = |2x - 48| - 1.652$ using the range setting indicated below. Your graph should appear as follows.

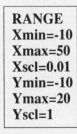

```
RANGE
Xmin=-10
Xmax=50
Xscl=0.01
Ymin=-10
Ymax=20
Yscl=1
```

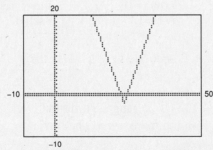

Next, save the range values by executing the program **RANGESAV**. The solutions of the equation $|2x - 48| - 1.652 = 0$ are the x-intercepts of the graph of $y = |2x - 48| - 1.652$. Zoom-in near the first solution until you obtain an estimate that is accurate to 0.01. (You should have to zoom-in about 5 times.) You should obtain a solution of 23.17. To find the second solution, you can first execute the program **RECALRNG** to obtain the original screen. Then zoom-in near the second solution until you obtain an estimate that is accurate to 0.01. You should obtain 24.83.

Problem Solving Using a Graphing Calculator

The zoom features on a graphing calculator can be used to estimate solutions of an equation. Whenever the zoom features are used, however, the range values are lost. The programs **RANGESAV** and **RECALRNG** are used to save range values and retrieve them after one or more zooms.

On this worksheet, you are asked to solve equations by using the following steps.

1. Find the range values such that each solution is visible on the screen.
2. Save the range values using the program **RANGESAV**.
3. Zoom in to estimate a solution to the nearest hundredth.
4. Recall the saved range values using the program **RECALRNG**.
5. Review the graph.
6. Repeat steps 3–5 until all solutions are found.

EXERCISES

1. Write the two-variable equation whose x-intercepts are solutions of $3x^3 + 4.4x^2 - 14x + 6.1 = 0$.

2. Which of the following range settings shows all the solutions of the equation in Exercise 1?

a.
```
RANGE
Xmin=0
Xmax=4
Xscl=0.01
Ymin=-10
Ymax=10
Yscl=1
```

b.
```
RANGE
Xmin=-4
Xmax=4
Xscl=0.01
Ymin=-10
Ymax=30
Yscl=1
```

c.
```
RANGE
Xmin=-4
Xmax=0
Xscl=0.01
Ymin=-30
Ymax=10
Yscl=1
```

d.
```
RANGE
Xmin=0
Xmax=30
Xscl=0.01
Ymin=0
Ymax=30
Yscl=1
```

3. Find all solutions of the equation in Exercise 1, accurate to 0.01. Use the six-step procedure outlined above.

4. Graph the equation $y = -0.03x^2 - 2.8x + 10$. Use a range setting that shows all x-intercepts and copy your results in the blank screen below.

5. Find all x-intercepts of the equation in Exercise 4 accurate to 0.01.

*Exploration Using a
Graphing Calculator*

(See Exercises 9–16 and 21–24
on page 318 of the text.)

This demonstration and worksheet can be used for group instruction
or by individual students with graphing calculators. On their
worksheets, students are asked to examine relationships of translated
and reflected graphs to simpler graphs.

<u>**EXAMPLE**</u>   **DESCRIBING TRANSLATIONS OF GRAPHS**

Graph each function and describe its relationship to the graph of a simpler function.

a. $g(x) = \sqrt{x} + 4$ **b.** $g(x) = (x - 3)^3$ **c.** $g(x) = -|x| - 1$

SOLUTION

a. The graph of $g(x) = \sqrt{x} + 4$ can be obtained by shifting the graph of
$f(x) = \sqrt{x}$ up 4 units.

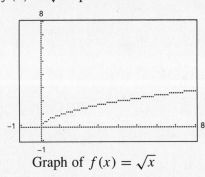

Graph of $f(x) = \sqrt{x}$

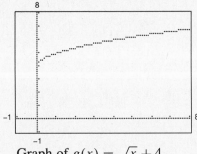

Graph of $g(x) = \sqrt{x} + 4$

b. The graph of $g(x) = (x - 3)^3$ can be obtained by shifting the graph of
$f(x) = x^3$ to the right 3 units.

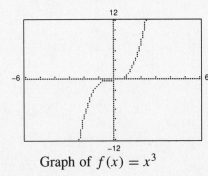

Graph of $f(x) = x^3$

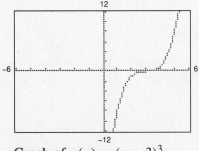

Graph of $g(x) = (x - 3)^3$

c. The graph of $g(x) = -|x| - 1$ can be obtained by reflecting the graph of
$f(x) = |x|$ in the x-axis and then shifting the result down 1 unit.

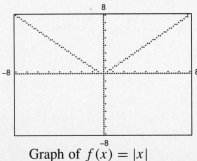

Graph of $f(x) = |x|$

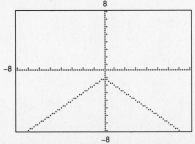

Graph of $g(x) = -|x| - 1$

6.5

Name _____

Exploration Using a Graphing Calculator

On this worksheet you are asked to use a graphing calculator to examine graphs of functions that are transformations of graphs of simpler functions.

EXERCISES

In Exercises 1–4, write the equation of the graph.

1. $y =$ _____

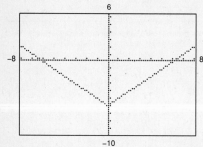

2. $y =$ _____

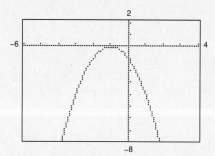

3. $y =$ _____

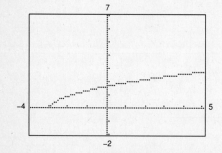

4. $y =$ _____

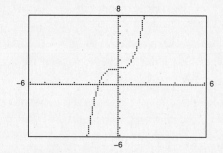

In Exercises 5–12, describe the transformation. Then graph the function. Copy your graph in the blank box.

5. $y = -x^2 - 3$

_____

_____

6. $y = |x + 4|$

_____

_____

7. $y = \sqrt{x} - 2$

_____

_____

8. $y = (x - 1)^2 + 1$

_____

_____

9. $y = -|x - 2|$

_____

_____

10. $y = (x + 1)^3$

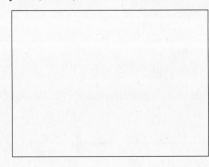

_____

_____

11. $y = -\sqrt{x + 1}$

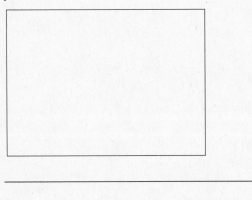

_____

_____

12. $y = -(x + 2)^2 + 3$

_____

_____

*Problem Solving Using
a Graphing Calculator*

This demonstration and worksheet can be used for group instruction or by individual students with graphing calculators. On their worksheets, students are asked to find the measures of central tendency for different collections of data.

The objective of the demonstration and worksheet is to help students understand the differences between the mean, median, and mode of a collection of data.

EXAMPLE   COMPARING MEASURES OF CENTRAL TENDENCY

Use a graphing calculator to construct a histogram for the following data.

4, 2, 5, 3, 5, 0, 4, 2, 1, 5, 3, 2, 5, 2, 3, 0, 2

Determine the **(a)** mean, **(b)** median, and **(c)** mode of the data.

SOLUTION

Begin by setting the range.

Xmin=0	**Xmax=6**	**Xscl=1**
Ymin=0	**Ymax=6**	**Yscl=1**

Next, enter the data into the graphing calculator and sketch the histogram. You should obtain the display shown below.

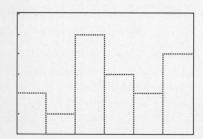

a. To determine the *mean* of the data, press the following.

TI-81:   2nd STAT 1 ENTER

CASIO fx-7700G: MODE × F4 F1 EXE

You should obtain a mean of 2.824. (Note that the data consists of 17 numbers.)

b. To determine the *median*, sort the data*, then enter the **EDIT** mode. The median is the 9th number in the list, which implies that the median is 3.

c. To determine the *mode*, redisplay the histogram and locate the number with the greatest frequency. For this data, the mode is 2.

* For the *Casio fx-7700G*, you must sort the data by hand. For the *TI-81*, you can sort the data by entering the following keystrokes.

2nd STAT ◁ 3 ENTER

*Problem Solving Using
a Graphing Calculator*

On this worksheet, you are asked to analyze a collection of data
by drawing a histogram of the data *and* by computing the mean,
median, and mode of the data.

EXERCISES

1. Use a graphing calculator to construct a
histogram for the following data. After
you have drawn the histogram, sketch the
result on the blank screen at the right.

   4, 6, 1, 7, 2, 4, 6, 1, 4, 3
   5, 4, 0, 2, 1, 3, 6, 1, 7, 4

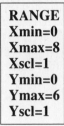

RANGE
Xmin=0
Xmax=8
Xscl=1
Ymin=0
Ymax=6
Yscl=1

2. Which value of x has the greatest frequency? What does this tell you about the mode of the data?

3. Use your graphing calculator to compute the mean of the data.

4. What is the median of the data?

5. Which of the three measures of central tendency do you think is most representative of this data?
Explain your reasoning.

6. Use a graphing calculator to sketch a
histogram for the following data. What
is the mean of this data?

   7, 3, 7, 0, 1, 4, 5, 8, 2, 7
   3, 4, 0, 8, 6, 7, 1, 5, 4, 7
   0, 5, 3, 7, 4, 2, 1, 5, 8, 0
   6, 4, 7, 3, 8, 6, 4, 1, 0, 5

RANGE
Xmin=0
Xmax=9
Xscl=1
Ymin=0
Ymax=7
Yscl=1

7.2

Exploration Using a Graphing Calculator

Program **GUESSEXP** is a game that can be played in a group instruction setting or on individual student graphing calculators. In either setting, the students should use the accompanying worksheet. (To save programming time, you may want to give the program to the students 1 or 2 days before you plan to use the activity in class.)

On their worksheets, students are asked to guess the values of C, R, and V in the equation $y = C(1 + R)^x + V$. When the program is executed, it randomly assigns values to the constants C, R and V: C is a multiple of 5 such that $5 \leq C \leq 25$, R is a multiple of 0.02 such that $-0.26 \leq R \leq 0.26$, and V is an integer such that $-2 \leq V \leq 1$. The program then displays the graph of $y = C(1 + R)^x + V$. Note that after each guess, the program displays the original graph and the graph that corresponds to the guessed values of C, R, and V.

TI-81 PROGRAM

```
Prgm1:GUESSEXP
:Disp "Yscl=10"
:5(IPart 5Rand+1)→C
:0.02(IPart 27Rand−13)→R
:IPart 4Rand−2→V
:"C(1+R)^X+V"→Y₁
:1→G
:Lbl 1
:ClrHome
:""→Y₂
:DispGraph
```

```
:Pause
:Disp "GUESS NUMBER"
:Disp G
:Disp "C="
:Input D
:Disp "R="
:Input E
:Disp "V="
:Input F
:"D(1+E)^X+F"→Y₂
```

```
:DispGraph
:Pause
:If (C=D)(R=E)(V=F)=1
:Goto 2
:G+1→G
:Goto 1
:Lbl 2
:Disp "CORRECT! NUMBER"
:Disp "OF GUESSES IS"
:Disp G
```

CASIO fx-7700G PROGRAM

```
GUESSEXP
5(Int 5Ran#+1)→C
0.02(Int 27Ran#−13)→R
Int 4Ran#−2→V
0→G
Lbl 1
Cls
G+1→G
Graph y= C(1+R)xʸX+V◢
"GUESS NUMBER"
```

```
G◢
"C="
?→D
"R="
?→E
"V="
?→F
Graph y=D(1+E)xʸX+F◢
0→X
0→Y
```

```
0→Z
C=D⇒1→X
R=E⇒1→Y
V=F⇒1→Z
XYZ→W
W≠ 1 ⇒Goto 1
"CORRECT! NUMBER"
"OF GUESSES IS"
G◢
```

This game is designed to allow students to discover that $C + V$ is the y-intercept of the graph of $y = C(1 + R)^x + V$ and that R determines whether the graph increases or decreases.

Before running the program, set the range as shown at the right. Also, for the *TI-81*, clear the $\boxed{Y=}$ screen, and set the grid mode to **Grid On**.

```
RANGE
Xmin=-9
Xmax=9
Xscl=1
Ymin=-10
Ymax=50
Yscl=10
```

Here is a sample game using the **GUESSEXP** program. The student guessed the correct values in 4 tries. The correct values for this game are $C = 20$, $R = -0.2$, and $V = -1$. Notice that the first and last displays contain only one graph.

Original Graph

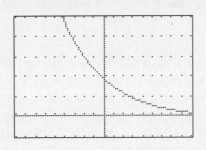

```
Yscl=10
GUESS NUMBER
                    1

C=
?-5
R=
?0.20
V=
?1
```

1st Guess

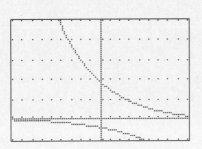

```
GUESS NUMBER
                    2

C=
?10
R=
?0.20
V=
?-1
```

2nd Guess

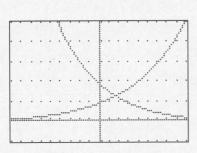

```
GUESS NUMBER
                    3

C=
?20
R=
?0.20
V=
?-1
```

3rd Guess

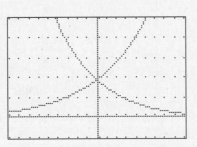

```
GUESS NUMBER
                    4

C=
?20
R=
?-0.20
V=
?-1
```

4th Guess

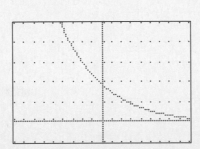

```
CORRECT! NUMBER
OF GUESSES IS

                    4
```

7.2

Name _____

Exploration Using a Graphing Calculator

Use the program **GUESSEXP** on a graphing calculator to complete each game.

1. Run the program. It will display the graph of an equation of the form $y = C(1 + R)^x + V$. Your goal is use the graph to guess the values of C, R, and V. C is a multiple of 5 such that $5 \leq C \leq 25$, R is a multiple of 0.02 such that $-0.26 \leq R \leq 0.26$, and V is an integer such that $-2 \leq V \leq 1$.

2. Write your guesses in the spaces provided below. Press ENTER or EXE. Then enter your guesses into the calculator, pressing ENTER or EXE after each value.

3. The calculator will display the original graph and the graph of your guess. If both graphs are the same, then your guess is correct. Press ENTER or EXE.

4. If your guess is incorrect, press ENTER or EXE. The calculator will display the original graph. Continue guessing until you find the correct values.

5. Sketch the correct graph and write the correct equation. Describe the effects of C, R, and V on the graph.

GAME 1	GAME 2	GAME 3
Guesses	**Guesses**	**Guesses**
C R V	C R V	C R V
1. ___ ___ ___	1. ___ ___ ___	1. ___ ___ ___
2. ___ ___ ___	2. ___ ___ ___	2. ___ ___ ___
3. ___ ___ ___	3. ___ ___ ___	3. ___ ___ ___
4. ___ ___ ___	4. ___ ___ ___	4. ___ ___ ___
5. ___ ___ ___	5. ___ ___ ___	5. ___ ___ ___
6. ___ ___ ___	6. ___ ___ ___	6. ___ ___ ___
7. ___ ___ ___	7. ___ ___ ___	7. ___ ___ ___
8. ___ ___ ___	8. ___ ___ ___	8. ___ ___ ___
Graph:	**Graph:**	**Graph:**

Equation: _____   **Equation:** _____   **Equation:** _____

Patterns:

Problem Solving Using a Graphing Calculator

This demonstration and worksheet can be used for group instruction or by individual students with graphing calculators.

With a graphing calculator, students can fit an exponential model of the form $y = a(b)^x$ to a set of data.

The objective of this activity is to help students develop a better understanding of exponential decay and half-life.

EXAMPLE WRITING A HALF-LIFE MODEL FOR REAL-LIFE DATA

For 1980 through 1992, the estimated number of elephants, y (in thousands), is given in the table. Find an exponential model for this data. Then approximate the half-life of the African elephant population.

Year	1980	1981	1982	1983	1984	1985	1986
y	1.20	1.12	1.04	0.97	0.91	0.84	0.79

Year	1987	1988	1989	1990	1991	1992
y	0.73	0.68	0.64	0.59	0.55	0.52

SOLUTION

To begin, let $x = 0$ represent 1980. Then enter the eleven data points into a graphing calculator. (Use the indicated range setting to obtain the scatter plot shown at the right.) Next, find the equation of the exponential model that best fits the data.

TI-81: ⬚2nd⬚ ⬚STAT⬚ ⬚4⬚ ⬚ENTER⬚

CASIO fx-7700G: ⬚MODE⬚ ⬚6⬚ ⬚F6⬚ ⬚F6⬚ ⬚F1⬚ ⬚EXE⬚ ⬚F2⬚ ⬚EXE⬚ ⬚F3⬚ ⬚EXE⬚

```
RANGE
Xmin=0
Xmax=12
Xscl=1
Ymin=0
Ymax=1.2
Yscl=0.1
```

For this data, you should obtain $a \approx 1.2$, $b \approx 0.932$, and $r \approx -1.00$. (On the *Casio*, the given B must be exponentiated to obtain the value of b for the form $y = a(b)^x$.)

$$y = 1.2(0.932)^x \qquad \textit{Exponential Model}$$

Note that this models implies that the elephant population is decreasing at the rate of about 6.8% per year.

To find the half-life for this model, you can sketch the graph of $y = 0.6$ on the same screen as the graph of the exponential model. Then, using the trace feature, you can approximate the half-life to be about 9.85 years.

You may want to ask students to compare the best-fitting linear model for this data with the best-fitting exponential model.

$$y = 1.153 - 0.0565x \qquad \textit{Linear Model}$$

These two models can be compared graphically on the same calculator screen.

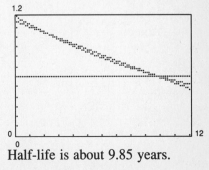

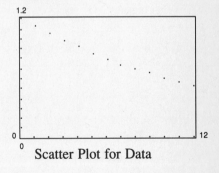

Scatter Plot for Data

Half-life is about 9.85 years.

7.2

Name _____

Problem Solving Using a Graphing Calculator

For this worksheet, you are asked to enter real-life data into a graphing calculator and find the best-fitting exponential model for the data. You are then asked to find the half-life of the exponential model.

EXERCISES

In Exercises 1–8, use the following information.

You bought a car for $14,280. One year later, the value of the car is assessed to be $11,200. Two years after you bought the car, its value is assessed to be $8900. After you have owned the car for five years, you sell it for $4300.

1. From the information about the value of your car, you can write four ordered pairs. What are they? (Let $x = 0$ represent the year you bought the car.)

2. Find the best-fitting linear model and the best-fitting exponential model for the four points.

   Linear Model

   a = _____

   b = _____

   r = _____

   Equation: _____

   Exponential Model

   a = _____

   b = _____

   r = _____

   Equation: _____

3. Which of the models in Exercise 2 do you think fits the data better? Explain your reasoning.

4. Sketch a scatter plot for the data. Choose appropriate range values and sketch the results below.

   RANGE
   Xmin=_____
   Xmax=_____
   Xscl=_____
   Ymin=_____
   Ymax=_____
   Yscl=_____

5. Draw the graphs of both models on the same screen that the scatter plot is drawn. Sketch the results below. Visually, which model do you think fits the data better? Does your conclusion agree with the conclusion you reached in Exercise 3?

6. The half-life of the value of your car is the number of years it takes for the value to drop to half of the original value. Draw the graph of the exponential model. Then, use the trace feature to approximate the half-life of the car's value. Make your approximation accurate to the nearest tenth of a year. (You may have to use the zoom feature.)

7. An exponential decay model of the form $y = a(b)^x$ can be written in **half-life form**

$$y = a \cdot (\tfrac{1}{2})^{x/h}$$

where h is the half-life. Use the result of Exercise 6 to write a half-life model for the value of your car.

8. Use the half-life model you found in Exercise 7 to find the number of years it takes for the car's value to reach the following.

a. Half of the original value. _____

b. One quarter of the original value. _____

c. $1000 _____

d. $500 _____

Problem Solving Using a Graphing Calculator

This demonstration and worksheet can be used for group instruction or by individual students with a graphing calculator.

The objective of the demonstration and worksheet is to help students understand how to use a graphing calculator to solve a radical equation.

EXAMPLE SOLVING A RADICAL EQUATION

Use a graphing calculator to solve $\sqrt{2x - 3} = 8$.

SOLUTION:

You can solve the equation graphically by first rewriting it as

$$\sqrt{2x - 3} - 8 = 0$$

and then approximating the x-intercept of $y = \sqrt{2x - 3} - 8$.

RANGE
Xmin=-10
Xmax=60
Xscl=0.1
Ymin=-10
Ymax=10
Yscl=1

To begin, set the range as shown at the right. Enter the equation and draw the graph. You should obtain the display shown below at the left. After zooming in four times (with a zoom factor of 4), you can obtain the display shown below at the right. From that display, you can approximate the solution to be $x \approx 33.5$. This can be checked algebraically as follows.

$$\sqrt{2(33.5) - 3} = \sqrt{64} = 8$$

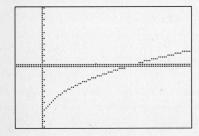

Original Graph

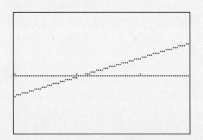

After Zooming In 4 Times

EXAMPLE AN EQUATION WITH NO SOLUTION

Use a graphing calculator to solve $5 - \sqrt{3x + 7} = 9$.

SOLUTION:

Use the range setting given by $-6 \le x \le 10$ and $-6 \le y \le 10$. Enter the equation

$$y = \sqrt{3x + 7} + 4.$$

Then draw the graph. From the display, you will see that the graph has no x-intercept. Therefore, the equation has no (real number) solution.

Problem Solving Using a Graphing Calculator

On this worksheet, you will be asked to solve radical equations with a graphing calculator. Remember that the basic procedure for doing this is to write the equation in the form

$$y = \text{left side} - \text{right side}$$

and then zoom in to approximate the x-intercept (or intercepts) of the graph. Before drawing the graph, remember to set the $Xscl$ to the desired accuracy.

EXERCISES

1. Use a graphing calculator to approximate the solution of

$$\sqrt{5x} - 9 = 2.$$

Zoom in as many times as needed to insure that your approximation is within one tenth of the actual solution.

a. Write the radical equation whose graph you used to approximate the solution of the given equation.

_____

b. Describe the range setting you used to obtain your first view of the graph. Then copy the first view in the blank screen at the right.

_____

c. What is the solution of the equation?

_____

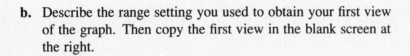

2. Use a graphing calculator to approximate the solution of

$$12 = 9 + 2\sqrt{\tfrac{3}{2}x + 1}.$$

Zoom in as many times as needed to insure that your approximation is within one tenth of the actual solution.

a. Write the radical equation whose graph you used to approximate the solution of the given equation.

_____

b. Describe the range setting you used to obtain your first view of the graph. Then copy the first view in the blank screen at the right.

_____

c. What is the solution of the equation?

_____

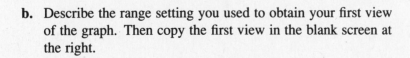

8.5

Problem Solving Using a Graphing Calculator

This demonstration and worksheet can be used for group instruction or by individual students with a graphing calculator. On their worksheets students are asked to use a graphing calculator to determine the best-fitting logarithmic equation of the form $y = a + b \ln x$ that models a collection of data.

The objective of the demonstration and worksheet is to help students understand how to use a graphing calculator to find a model.

EXAMPLE FINDING A BEST-FITTING LOGARITHMIC MODEL

Find the best-fitting logarithmic equation that relates the average surface temperature, y (in degrees Celsius), of a planet and the average distance, x (in millions of kilometers), from the sun.

Planet	Mercury	Venus	Earth	Mars	Jupiter	Saturn	Uranus	Neptune	Pluto
Distance, x	58	108	150	228	778	1430	2875	4504	5900
Temperature, y	127	462	-16	-63	-148	-178	-216	-214	-228

SOLUTION:

To begin, clear all statistical memory that may be stored in your calculator. Also, on the *TI-81*, clear the [Y=] screen. Enter the nine data points given in the table into the graphing calculator. Use the indicated range setting to obtain the scatter plot shown below at the left. Next, find the logarithmic equation that best fits the data.

RANGE
Xmin=0
Xmax=6000
Xscl=1000
Ymin=-500
Ymax=200
Yscl=100

TI-81: [2nd] [STAT] [3] [ENTER]

CASIO fx-7700G: [MODE] [5] [F6] [F6] [F1] [EXE] [F2] [EXE] [F3] [EXE]

For this data, you should obtain $a \approx 615.4$, $b \approx -103.4$, and $r \approx -0.790$. Therefore, the best-fitting logarithmic model is

$$y = 615.4 - 103.4 \ln x.$$

The screen below at the right shows the graph of this logarithmic model with the scatter plot.

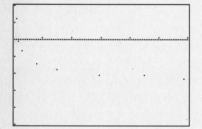

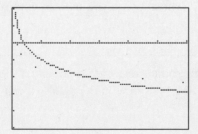

Problem Solving Using a Graphing Calculator

On this worksheet, you are asked to use a graphing calculator to find the best-fitting logarithmic model of a collection of data.

EXERCISES

1. The annual sales, y (in millions of dollars), of a company from 1982 to 1990 is given in the table.

Year	1982	1983	1984	1985	1986	1987	1988	1989	1990
Sales	12.0	14.4	19.1	19.9	22.4	22.9	23.9	26.1	26.6

   Use the following steps with a graphing calculator to find the logarithmic model that best fits this data. (Let x represent the year with $x = 2$ corresponding to 1982.)

   a. Use an appropriate range setting to graph a scatter plot of the data. Copy the results in the blank screen below.

   b. Find the logarithmic equation that best fits the data.

   TI-81: 2nd STAT 3 ENTER

   CASIO fx-7700G: MODE 5 F6 F6 F1 EXE F2 EXE F3 EXE

   c. Graph the model and the scatter plot on the same screen. Copy your results in the blank screen below.

   Scatter plot   Scatter plot with graph

2. For 1983 through 1989, the total imports, y (in millions of dollars), of footwear in the United States are given in the table.

Year	1983	1984	1985	1986	1987	1988	1989
Imports	4010	5034	5695	6473	7236	8041	8393

   Find the logarithmic model that best fits this data. (Let x represent the year with $x = 3$ corresponding to 1983.)

3. Use the model in Exercise 2 to predict the total imports of footwear in 1996.

Problem Solving Using a Graphing Calculator

(See Exercises 47–50 on page 439 of the text.)

This demonstration and worksheet can be used for group instruction or by individual students with a graphing calculator. On their worksheets students are asked to use a graphing calculator to solve exponential equations of the form $Ce^{bx} = d$.

EXAMPLE SOLVING AN EXPONENTIAL EQUATION GRAPHICALLY

You have deposited $1000 in a savings account the pays 6% annual interest, compounded continuously. Without making any additional deposits, how long will it take your balance to double? To triple?

SOLUTION:

The formula for the balance in the account is $A = Pe^{rt}$, where $P = 1000$ is the initial deposit and $r = 0.06$ is the annual interest rate. For the balance to double, you must find the value of t for which $2000 = 1000e^{0.06t}$. This equation could be solved algebraically as discussed in Lesson 8.6. It could also be solved graphically by finding the point of intersection of the graphs of

$$A = 2000 \quad \text{and} \quad A = 1000e^{0.06t}.$$

To do this, sketch both graphs on the same screen, using the indicated range setting. By zooming in near the point of intersection, you can determine that the balance will double in approximately 11.6 years.

RANGE
Xmin=0
Xmax=14
Xscl=1
Ymin=0
Ymax=2500
Yscl=500

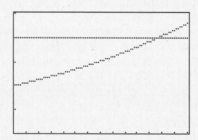

To find the time required for the balance to triple, sketch the graphs of $A = 3000$ and $A = 1000e^{0.06t}$ on the same screen, as shown below. By zooming in near the point of intersection, you can determine that the balance will triple in approximately 18.3 years.

RANGE
Xmin=0
Xmax=20
Xscl=1
Ymin=0
Ymax=3500
Yscl=500

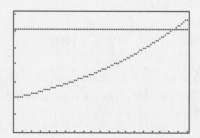

8.6

Name _____

*Problem Solving Using
a Graphing Calculator*

On this worksheet, you are asked to solve exponential equations
graphically. For instance, to solve the exponential equation
$Ce^{bx} = d$, you can graph $y = d$ and $y = Ce^{bx}$ on the same screen
and zoom in to approximate the point of intersection.

EXERCISES

1. The air pressure, P, at sea level is about 14.7 pounds per square inch.
   As the altitude, h (in feet above sea level), increases, the air pressure
   decreases. The relationship between air pressure and altitude can be
   modeled by

   $$P = 14.7e^{-0.00004h}.$$

   At the top of Pikes Peak, in Colorado, the air pressure is about 8.36
   pounds per square inch. What is the altitude at the top of the peak? To
   answer this question, use the following steps.

   a. Sketch the graphs of $P = 8.36$ and $P = 14.7e^{-0.00004h}$ on the same
   screen. Copy the results in the blank screen below.

   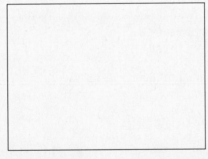

   ```
   RANGE
   Xmin=0
   Xmax=20000
   Xscl=100
   Ymin=0
   Ymax=15
   Yscl=1
   ```

   b. Use the zoom feature of your graphing calculator to approximate the
   point of intersection of the two graphs.

   c. Solve the equation $8.36 = 14.7e^{-0.00004h}$ algebraically. How does the
   result compare with that obtained graphically?

2. You have deposited $1000 in a savings account that pays 7%, compounded
   continuously. How long will it take your balance to double? Is it possible
   that the balance in the account would ever reach $1 million? Justify your
   answers graphically in the blank screens below.

   Time for balance to double   Time for balance to reach $1 million

*Problem Solving Using
a Graphing Calculator*

(See Exercises 55 and 56 on
page 469 of the text.)

This demonstration and worksheet can be used for group instruction or by individual students with a graphing calculator. On their worksheets students are asked to determine equations for the volumes of a rectangular solid and a cylinder. Then, students are asked to use a graphing calculator to find the dimensions that produce a maximum volume.

The objective of this demonstration and worksheet is for students to understand that mathematics can be used to help make decisions about the use of scarce resources.

EXAMPLE THE BOX PROBLEM

Imagine that you are in a decision-making position at a corporation. One of your responsibilities is to design a box for storing a product. The constraints are as follows.

- The box must be cut from an $8\frac{1}{2}$-inch by 11-inch piece of cardboard.
- To form the box, four congruent squares are cut out, one from each corner.
- The sides are then folded up to form an open box.
- The volume must be maximized by choosing dimensions for the squares that are accurate to the nearest 0.01 inch.

SOLUTION:

To begin, try an example. For instance, if one-inch squares are cut from each corner, then the dimensions of the box are

Length: 9 in.   Width: $6\frac{1}{2}$ in.   Height: 1 in.

This box has a volume of $(9)(6\frac{1}{2})(1) = 58.5$ cubic inches. In general, if a square having sides of x inches are cut from each corner, then the dimensions of the box are

Length: $11 - 2x$ in.   Width: $8\frac{1}{2} - 2x$ in.   Height: x in.

The volume of this box is $V = (11 - 2x)(8\frac{1}{2} - 2x)(x)$ cubic inches. By graphing this equation and using the zoom and trace keys, you can observe that the maximum volume occurs when x is about 1.59 inches.

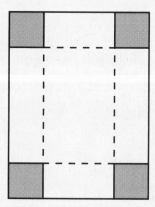

$8\frac{1}{2}$ inch by 11 inch
Cut squares from corners.

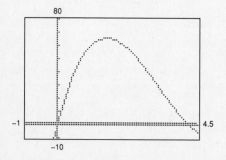

ⓒ D.C. Heath and Company

Problem Solving Using
a Graphing Calculator

One reason for studying mathematics is to be equipped to make decisions that optimize (either minimize or maximize) the use of scarce resources. Graphing calculators allow you to solve optimization problems that would otherwise be reserved for a course in calculus.

On this worksheet, you are asked to use a graphing calculator to make decisions that maximize the volume of an object made from a scarce resource.

EXERCISES

1. An open box is formed by cutting four congruent squares from the corners of an 18-inch by 21-inch piece of cardboard and folding up the sides. Each cut out square has sides of x inches. Which of the following functions represents the volume, y (in cubic inches), of the box?

   a. $y = (21 - 2x)(18 - 2x)(x)$ **b.** $y = (21 - x)(18 - x)(x)$

   c. $x = (21 - 2y)(18 - 2y)(y)$ **d.** $y = (21 - 4x)(18 - 4x)(x)$

2. The screen at the right shows the graph of

   $$y = (30 - 2x)(20 - 2x)(x).$$

   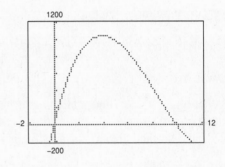

   This function represents the volume of an open box made from a 30-inch by 20-inch piece of aluminum. To form the box, x by x squares are cut from each corner and the sides are folded up. Answer true or false to each statement. (To help answer the questions, graph the equation on your graphing calculator and use the zoom and trace features.)

   a. The horizontal axis represents the length of each of the four cut-out squares.

   b. The horizontal axis represents the volume of the open box.

   c. To obtain a maximum volume, squares of about 3.927 inches by 3.927 inches should be cut from each corner.

   d. If the squares have sides of about 1056.31 inches, the volume will be about 3.927 cubic inches.

   e. If the squares have sides of about 3.927 inches, the volume will be about 1056.31 cubic inches.

   f. The maximum possible volume is about 1056.31 cubic inches.

   g. If x increases, y will increase.

   h. If the square length decreases, the volume will increase.

   i. If the square length increases, the volume will increase.

3. Find an equation for the volume, y (in cubic inches), of an open box that is created from a 15-inch by 24-inch sheet of cardboard.

4. Sketch the graph of the volume model you found in Exercise 3. Choose a range setting that gives a reasonable view of the graph (for the context of the problem). Copy the result in the blank screen below.

5. Use the zoom and trace features of your graphing calculator to approximate the maximum volume of the box in Exercise 3. What size squares should be cut out to produce this maximum volume?

6. An aluminum soft drink can is 12 centimeters tall and has a radius of 3.25 centimeters. Its volume, V (in cubic centimeters), and surface area, S (in square centimeters), are

$$V = \pi(3.25)^2(12) \approx 398.2 \text{ cm}^3$$

and

$$S = 2\pi(3.25)^2 + 2\pi(3.25)(12) \approx 311.4 \text{ cm}^2.$$

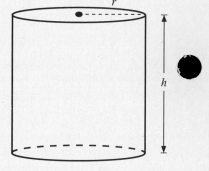

Is it possible to create a cylindrical can that has the same surface area, but has a greater volume? To answer this question, note that the volume, V, and surface area, S, of a cylinder is

$$V = \pi r^2 h \quad \text{and} \quad S = 311.4 = 2\pi r^2 + 2\pi r h.$$

Solving for h in the second equation and substituting into the first equation produces

$$V = \pi r^2 \left(\frac{311.4 - 2\pi r^2}{2\pi r} \right).$$

Use a graphing calculator to find a value of r that produces a volume that is greater than 398.2 cubic centimeters. What is the maximum volume that can be obtained by varying the radius (while keeping the same surface area)?

Problem Solving Using a Graphing Calculator

This demonstration and worksheet can be used for group instruction or by individual students with a graphing calculator. On their worksheets students are asked to write polynomials that have given x-intercepts and then verify the result with a graphing calculator.

The objective of this demonstration and worksheet is for students to understand the relationship between the factors of a polynomial and the x-intercepts of its graph.

EXAMPLE WRITING A POLYNOMIAL WITH GIVEN INTERCEPTS

Write an equation of a third-degree polynomial function whose x-intercepts are -1, 2, and 3.

SOLUTION

By the Zero Product Property, you know that

$$(x - (-1)), (x - 2), \text{ and } (x - 3)$$

are factors of the polynomial. Therefore, one possible equation is

$$y = (x + 1)(x - 2)(x - 3) = x^3 - 4x^2 + x + 6.$$

You can verify this result graphically by sketching the graph of the polynomial as shown below. From the screen, notice that the graph crosses the x-axis when $x = -1$, $x = 2$, and $x = 3$.

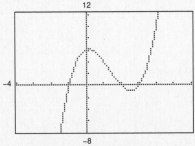

This is not the only third-degree polynomial function that has these three x-intercepts. Any constant multiple of the polynomial has the same three intercepts. For instance, the three graphs shown below all have the same x-intercepts.

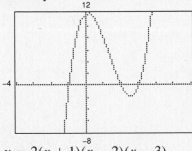

$$y = 2(x + 1)(x - 2)(x - 3)$$

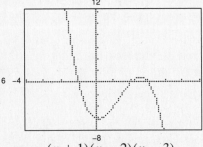

$$y = -(x + 1)(x - 2)(x - 3)$$

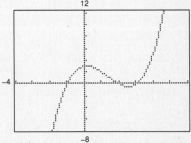

$$y = \tfrac{1}{2}(x + 1)(x - 2)(x - 3)$$

Problem Solving Using a Graphing Calculator

On this worksheet, you are asked to write equations of polynomials that have specified x-intercepts. For example, a third-degree polynomial that has -2, 1, and 4 as x-intercepts is

$$y = (x - (-2))(x - 1)(x - 4)$$
$$= (x + 2)(x - 1)(x - 4) \qquad \textit{Factor form}$$
$$= x^3 - 3x^2 - 6x + 8. \qquad \textit{Expanded form}$$

EXERCISES

1. Write an equation of a third-degree polynomial function that has -2, -1, and 3 as its x-intercepts. Write the result in factored form and expanded form. Then use a graphing calculator to sketch the graph of each. If you expanded correctly, each form will have the same graph. Sketch the graph in the blank screen at the right.

In Exercises 2–4, write an equation of the polynomial function whose graph is shown. Check your result by sketching the graph with a graphing calculator.

2.
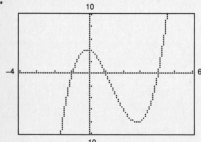

3.
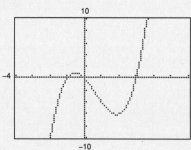

4.
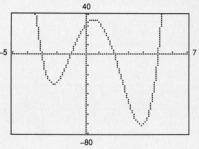

5. Which of the following third-degree polynomial functions have 1 and 2 as its only x-intercepts? Justify your conclusion by sketching the graph of each function.

   a. $y = (x - 1)(x - 2)^2$
   b. $y = (x - 1)^2(x - 2)$
   c. $y = 2(x - 1)(x - 2)^2$
   d. $y = -(x - 1)^2(x - 2)$

6. If the graph of a function has only one x-intercept, does that mean that the graph must "cross" the x-axis? Use the graph of $y = (x^2 + 1)(x - 2)^2$ to help form your conclusion.

7. Sketch the graphs of $y = (x - 2)^2$, $y = (x - 1)(x - 2)^2$, and $y = (x - 1)(x - 2)^2(x - 3)$. Does each graph "touch" the x-axis at $x = 2$ or "cross" the x-axis at $x = 2$?

Problem Solving Using a Spreadsheet

(See Exercises 19–30 on page 484 of the text.)

This demonstration and worksheet can be used for group instruction or by individual students with a spreadsheet. On their worksheets, students are asked to use a spreadsheet to perform synthetic division.

The objective of this demonstration and worksheet is for students to learn how to enter formulas into the locations of a spreadsheet.

EXAMPLE PERFORMING SYNTHETIC DIVISION

Use a spreadsheet to divide $x^4 - 10x^2 + 2x + 3$ by $x - 3$. (See Example 2 on page 481 of the text.)

SOLUTION

A spreadsheet can be used to solve this problem. You can begin by entering formulas into the spreadsheet locations as follows.

	A	B	C	D	E	F
1						
2			A1*B3	A1*C3	A1*D3	A1*E3
3		B1	C1+C2	D1+D2	E1+E2	F1+F2

After entering the above formulas, enter 3 in location A1 and enter the coefficients of the polynomial in locations B1, C1, D1, E1, and F1 as follows.

	A	B	C	D	E	F
1	3	1	0	-10	2	3
2			3	9	-3	-3
3		1	3	-1	-1	0

Synthetic Division Array

$$3 \,\underline{\begin{array}{|ccccc} 1 & 0 & -10 & 2 & 3 \\ & 3 & 9 & -3 & -3 \\ \hline 1 & 3 & -1 & -1 & 0 \end{array}}$$

Because the number in location F3 is 0, you can conclude that $x - 3$ divides evenly into $x^4 - 10x^2 + 2x + 3$. That is,

$$\frac{x^4 - 10x^2 + 2x + 3}{x - 3} = x^3 + 3x^2 - x - 1.$$

This spreadsheet can be used to divide *any* 3rd or 4th degree polynomial by a polynomial of the form $x - k$. The number k should be entered in location A1, and the coefficients of the polynomial should be entered in locations B1, C1, D1, E1, and F1. For cubic polynomials, enter 0 in location F1.

This spreadsheet technique is especially useful for testing the possible zeros given by the Rational Zero Test. For instance, try using this technique to test the possible rational zeros given in Example 2 on page 489 of the text.

Long Division Array

$$\begin{array}{r}
x^3 + 3x^2 - x - 1 \\
x - 3 \overline{\smash{)}x^4 - 10x^2 + 2x + 3} \\
\underline{x^4 - 3x^3} \\
3x^3 - 10x^2 \\
\underline{3x^3 - 9x^2} \\
-x^2 + 2x \\
\underline{-x^2 + 3x} \\
-x + 3 \\
\underline{-x + 3} \\
0
\end{array}$$

9.4

Name _____

Problem Solving
Using a Spreadsheet

On this worksheet, you are asked to use a spreadsheet to perform synthetic division.

EXERCISES

1. The following spreadsheet array is used to perform synthetic division. The numbers in locations A1, B1, C1, D1, E1, and F1 are as shown in the following quotient.

$$\frac{B1x^4 + C1x^3 + D1x^2 + E1x + F1}{x - A1} \quad \text{or} \quad \frac{B1x^3 + C1x^2 + D1x + E1}{x - A1}$$

Which formulas should go into the locations labeled with question marks? (For instance, the formula for location C2 is A1*B3.)

	A	B	C	D	E	F
1						
2			?	?	?	?
3		?	?	?	?	?

In Exercises 2 and 3, use the following spreadsheet.

	A	B	C	D	E	F
1	2	2	-7	7	-6	8
2			4	-6	2	-8
3		2	-3	1	-4	0

2. Which quotient is represented by the spreadsheet?

3. Write the corresponding long division array.

In Exercises 4–7, use a spreadsheet to perform the division.

4. $(x^4 + 3x^3 + x^2 + 1) \div (x + 1)$

5. $(3x^4 - 17x^3 + 10x^2 + x - 5) \div (x - 5)$

6. $(x^3 + 12x^2 + 22x - 15) \div (x + 3)$

7. $(-2x^3 + 15x^2 - 29x + 4) \div (x - 4)$

In Exercises 8 and 9, use synthetic division to determine which of the rational numbers are zeros of the function.

8. $f(x) = 2x^3 + x^2 - 7x - 6$
   $x = \pm 1, \ \pm 2, \ \pm\frac{3}{2}$

9. $f(x) = 3x^4 + 5x^3 - 13x^2 - 29x - 14$
   $x = \pm 1, \ \pm 2, \ \pm\frac{7}{3}$

In Exercises 10 and 11, use a spreadsheet and the Remainder Theorem to evaluate the function.

10. Evaluate $f(5)$ for $f(x) = 2x^3 + 5x^2 - 2x + 10$

11. Evaluate $f(-1)$ for $f(x) = 13x^4 + x^3 - 4x + 9$

*Problem Solving Using
a Graphing Calculator*

(See Exercises 11–20 on
page 491 of the text.)

This demonstration and worksheet can be used for group instruction or by individual students with a graphing calculator. Program **SYNTHDIV** performs synthetic division. (To save programming time, you may want to give the program to students 1 or 2 days before you plan to use the activity in class.)

On their worksheets, students are asked to first compare a list of possible rational zeros of a polynomial function to the graph of the function to shorten the list of possible rational zeros. Next students are asked to use program **SYNTHDIV** to determine the actual zeros. Finally, students are asked to write the polynomial function in factored form.

TI-81 PROGRAM

Prgm3: SYNTHDIV	:0→P	:RQ→S
:ClrHome	:Lbl 1	:Q→{y}(P)
:Lbl 0	:P+1→P	:P+1→P
:Disp "POSSIBLE ZERO"	:Disp "COEFFICIENT"	:If P≤D+1
:Input R	:Input C	:Goto 3
:Disp "COEFFICIENTS?"	:C→{x}(P)	:Goto 0
:Disp "0 = NEW"	:If P<D+1	:Lbl 4
:Disp "1 = QUOTIENT"	:Goto 1	:D−1→D
:Disp "2 = SAME"	:Lbl 2	:0→P
:Input W	:1→P	:Lbl 5
:If W=2	:0→S	:1+P→P
:Goto 2	:Lbl 3	:{y}(P)→{x}(P)
:If W=1	:{x}(P)→F	:If P<D+1
:Goto 4	:F+S→Q	:Goto 5
:Disp "DIVIDEND DEGREE"	:Disp Q	:Goto 2
:Input D	:Pause	

CASIO fx-7700G PROGRAM

SYNTHETIC DIVISION	0→P	RQ→S
Defm 40	Lbl 1	Q→Z[P+20]
Lbl 0	P+1→P	P+1→P
"POSSIBLE ZERO"	"COEFFICIENT"	P≤D+1⇒Goto 3
?→R	?→C	Goto 0
"COEFFICIENTS?"	C→Z[P]	Lbl 4
"0 = NEW"	P<D+1⇒Goto 1	D−1→D
"1 = QUOTIENT"	Lbl 2	0→P
"2 = SAME"	1→P	Lbl 5
?→W	0→S	1+P→P
W=2⇒Goto 2	Lbl 3	Z[P+20]→Z[P]
W=1⇒Goto 4	Z[P]→F	P<D+1⇒Goto 5
"DIVIDEND DEGREE"	F+S→Q	Goto 2
?→D	Q◢	

EXAMPLE TESTING POSSIBLE RATIONAL ZEROS

Find the exact zeros of $f(x) = 4x^4 - 24x^3 - 63x^2 + 349x - 156$ and use the result to write $f(x)$ in factored form.

SOLUTION

For this polynomial function, the list of possible rational zeros is overwhelming!

± 1, $\pm\frac{1}{2}$, $\pm\frac{1}{4}$, ± 2, ± 3, $\pm\frac{3}{2}$, $\pm\frac{3}{4}$, ± 4, ± 6, ± 12, ± 13, $\pm\frac{13}{2}$,

$\pm\frac{13}{4}$, ± 26, ± 39, $\pm\frac{39}{2}$, $\pm\frac{39}{4}$, ± 52, ± 78, ± 156

To shorten the list, it helps to first sketch the graph of f, as shown below. From the graph, it appears that -4, $\frac{1}{4}$, $\frac{1}{2}$, 3, and $\frac{13}{2}$ could be zeros. To test these, you can use the program **SYNTHDIV**. Suppose you begin by testing $\frac{1}{4}$. The output of the program is shown below.

```
POSSIBLE ZERO
?1/4
COEFFICIENTS?
0=NEW
1=QUOTIENT
2=SAME
?0
DIVIDEND DEGREE
?4
COEFFICIENT
?4
COEFFICIENT
?-24
COEFFICIENT
?-63
COEFFICIENT
?349
COEFFICIENT
?-156
                4
              -23
           -68.75
          331.8125
         -73.046875
```

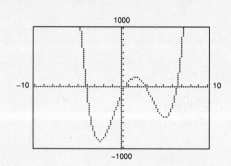

From the output, you can conclude that $\frac{1}{4}$ is not a zero of the polynomial. Now, try $\frac{1}{2}$, 3, $\frac{13}{2}$, and -4. From the output shown below, you can see that each is a zero of the polynomial. This implies that the factored form is

$$f(x) = (x - \tfrac{1}{2})(x - 3)(x - \tfrac{13}{2})(x + 4).$$

In the outputs shown below, notice that you do not have to reenter the coefficients to test a new zero. Also, notice that each time you find an actual zero, the degree of the quotient decreases by one.

```
POSSIBLE ZERO
?1/2
COEFFICIENTS?
0=NEW
1=QUOTIENT
2=SAME
?2
          4
        -22
        -74
        312
          0
```

```
POSSIBLE ZERO
?3
COEFFICIENTS?
0=NEW
1=QUOTIENT
2=SAME
?1
          4
        -10
       -104
          0
```

```
POSSIBLE ZERO
?13/2
COEFFICIENTS?
0=NEW
1=QUOTIENT
2=SAME
?1
          4
         16
          0
```

```
POSSIBLE ZERO
?-4
COEFFICIENTS?
0=NEW
1=QUOTIENT
2=SAME
?1
          4
          0
```

*Problem Solving Using
a Graphing Calculator*

Graphing calculators can be used to find the zeros of a polynomial function. On this worksheet, you are asked to use a graphing calculator in two ways.

1. First, you will compare a list of possible rational zeros to the graph of the function to obtain shorter list of possible rational zeros.

2. Second, you will use the program **SYNTHDIV** to identify which possible zeros from the shorter list are actual zeros.

EXERCISES

In Exercises 1–3, compare the list of possible rational zeros to the graph of the function. Make a shorter list of only those numbers that are consistent with the graph.

1. $y = 2x^3 + 5x^2 - 21x - 36$

   $\pm 1, \pm\frac{1}{2}, \pm 2, \pm 3, \pm\frac{3}{2}, \pm 4, \pm 6$

   $\pm 9, \pm\frac{9}{2}, \pm 12, \pm 18, \pm 36$

   Shortened List:

   _____

   _____

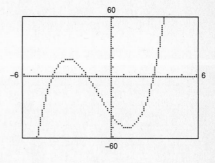

2. $y = 3x^4 + 19x^3 - 3x^2 - 139x - 120$

   $\pm 1, \pm\frac{1}{3}, \pm 2, \pm\frac{2}{3}, \pm 3, \pm 4, \pm\frac{4}{3}, \pm 5, \pm\frac{5}{3}$

   $\pm 6, \pm 8, \pm\frac{8}{3}, \pm 10, \pm\frac{10}{3}, \pm 12, \pm 15$

   $\pm 20, \pm\frac{20}{3}, \pm 24, \pm 30, \pm 40, \pm\frac{40}{3}, \pm 60, \pm 120$

   Shortened List:

   _____

   _____

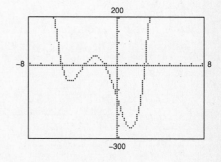

3. $y = 6x^3 - 13x^2 - 19x + 12$

   $\pm 1, \pm\frac{1}{2}, \pm\frac{1}{3}, \pm\frac{1}{6}, \pm 2, \pm\frac{2}{3}$

   $\pm 3, \pm\frac{3}{2}, \pm 4, \pm\frac{4}{3}, \pm 6, \pm 12$

   Shortened List:

   _____

   _____

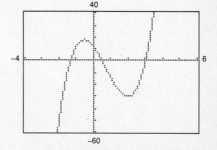

In Exercises 4–6, use the shortened list of possible rational zeros from Exercises 1–3 with the program **SYNTHDIV** to find all the actual real zero's of the polynomial function. Fill in the table as you work. When finished, write the function in factored form.

4. $y = 2x^3 + 5x^2 - 21x - 36$

Possible Roots (Exercise 1)	Coefficients? (0, 1, or 2)	Dividend Degree	Remainder	Quotient (If Remainder = 0)	Actual Zero? (Yes or No)

5. $y = 3x^4 + 19x^3 - 3x^2 - 139x - 120$

Possible Roots (Exercise 2)	Coefficients? (0, 1, or 2)	Dividend Degree	Remainder	Quotient (If Remainder = 0)	Actual Zero? (Yes or No)

6. $y = 6x^3 - 13x^2 - 19x + 12$

Possible Roots (Exercise 3)	Coefficients? (0, 1, or 2)	Dividend Degree	Remainder	Quotient (If Remainder = 0)	Actual Zero? (Yes or No)

7. Find all real zeros of

$$y = 6x^6 - 83x^5 + 108x^4 + 342x^3 - 678x^2 + 365x - 60.$$

To begin, sketch the graph of the function.

Exploration Using a Graphing Calculator

(See Exercises 12–19 on page 498 of the text.)

Program **CUBETUTR** is a game that can be played in a group-instruction setting or on individual students graphing calculators. (To save programming time, you may want to give the program to students 1 or 2 days before you plan to use the activity in class.)

On their worksheets, students are asked to determine the values of b, c, and d in the equation $(x - R)(x - S)(x - U) = x^3 + bx^2 + cx + d$. When the program is run, it randomly assigns values to the three constants R, S, and U: each is an integer between -6 and 6. The program then displays the graph of $y = (x - R)(x - S)(x - U)$. Based on R, S, and U (the x-intercepts of the graph), students are asked to find the values of b, c, and d by multiplying the factors.

The objective of this demonstration and worksheet is for students to understand the connection between x-intercepts of a graph and its cubic equation.

TI-81 PROGRAM

```
Prgm2: CUBETUTR
:Lbl 1
:IPart 13Rand−6→R
:IPart 13Rand−6→S
:IPart 13Rand−6→U
:If (R=S)+(S=U)+(R=U)≥1
:Goto 1
:"(X−R)(X−S)(X−U)"→Y₁
:Lbl 2
:DispGraph
:Pause
:Disp "(X−R)(X−S)(X−U)=0"
```

```
:Disp "X³+BX²+CX+D=0"
:Disp "B="
:Input B
:Disp "C="
:Input C
:Disp "D="
:Input D
:-(R+S+U)→E
:RS+SU+RU→F
:-RSU→G
:If (B=E)(C=F)(D=G)=1
:Goto 3
```

```
:Disp "TRY AGAIN"
:Pause
:Goto 2
:Lbl 3
:Disp "YOU DID IT!"
:Disp "R="
:Disp R
:Disp "S="
:Disp S
:Disp "U="
:Disp U
```

CASIO fx-7700G PROGRAM

```
CUBETUTOR
Lbl 1
Int 13Ran#−6→R
Int 13Ran#−6→S
Int 13Ran#−6→U
0→X: 0→Y: 0→Z
R=S⇒1→X
S=U⇒1→Y
R=U⇒1→A
X+Y+Z→W
W≥1⇒Goto 1
Lbl 2
Cls
Graph Y=(X−R)(X−S)(X−U)◢
```

```
"(X−R)(X−S)(X−U)=0"
"Xxʸ3+BX²+CX+D=0"
"B="
?→B
"C="
?→C
"D="
?→D
-(R+S+U)→E
RS+SU+RU→F
-RSU→G
0→X: 0→Y: 0→Z
B=E⇒1→X
C=F⇒1→Y
```

```
D=G⇒1→Z
XYZ→W
W=1⇒Goto 3
"TRY AGAIN"◢
Goto 2
Lbl 3
"YOU DID IT!"
"R="
R◢
"S="
S◢
"U="
U◢
```

Before running the program, set the range to the standard setting in which $-10 \le x \le 10$ and $-10 \le y \le 10$.

EXAMPLE   CONNECTING INTERCEPTS AND FACTORS

Solve $x^3 - 6x^2 + 5x + 12 = 0$ and interpret the solutions graphically.

SOLUTION

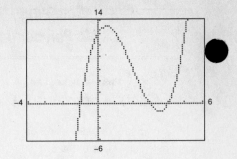

$$x^3 - 6x^2 + 5x + 12 = 0 \qquad \textit{Original equation}$$
$$(x + 1)(x - 3)(x - 4) = 0 \qquad \textit{Factor left side.}$$
$$x + 1 = 0 \implies x = -1 \qquad \textit{Let 1st factor equal 0.}$$
$$x - 3 = 0 \implies x = 3 \qquad \textit{Let 2nd factor equal 0.}$$
$$x - 4 = 0 \implies x = 4 \qquad \textit{Let 3rd factor equal 0.}$$

The solutions are -1, 3, and 4. Graphically, these solutions correspond to the x-intercepts of the graph of $y = x^3 - 6x^2 + 5x + 12$, as shown at the right.

In the example shown above, students are asked to solve a quadratic equation and then use the result to describe the x-intercepts. In the game **CUBETUTR**, students are asked to use the reverse process. That is, they are given a graph and are asked to write the quadratic equation that corresponds to the graph.

SAMPLE GAME

1. When the program is run, a graph like the one at the right will appear. From the graph, the player should determine that the intercepts are $R = -3$, $S = -1$, and $U = 4$.

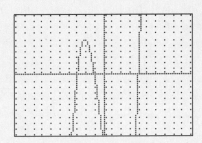

2. On a piece of paper, the player should write the following.

$$(x - R)(x - S)(x - U) = 0$$
$$(x - (-3))(x - (-1))(x - 4) = 0$$
$$(x + 3)(x + 1)(x - 4) = 0$$
$$x^3 - 13x - 12 = 0$$

Thus, $B = 0$, $C = -13$, and $D = -12$.

3. After determining the values of B, C, and D the player should press ENTER or EXE . After entering B, C, and D the program with confirm that the values are correct, as shown at the right.

If the player enters incorrect values for B, C, or D, then the program will display the message "TRY AGAIN." At this point, the player should press ENTER or EXE to continue the game.

```
Prgm2
(X−R)(X−S)(X−U)=0
X³+BX²+CX+D=0
B=
?0
C=
?-13
D=
?-12
YOU DID IT!
R=
                    -3
S=
                    -1
U=
                    4
```

Exploration Using a Graphing Calculator

Use the program **CUBETUTR** on a graphing calculator to complete each game.

1. Run the program. It will display the graph of an equation $y = x^3 + bx^2 + cx + d = (x - R)(x - S)(x - U)$. Sketch the graph on your gamesheet. Your goal is to use the x-intercepts (R, S, and U) to calculate b, c, and d.

2. Write the values for R, S, and U in the spaces provided on the gamesheet. Press ENTER or EXE. Then multiply to write the cubic $(x - R)(x - S)(x - U) = 0$ in the form $x^3 + bx^2 + cx + d = 0$.

3. Write the values of b, c, and d on your gamesheet. Then enter the values into the graphing calculator. If the values are correct, it will display the message "YOU DID IT!" If the values are incorrect, you can try again.

GAME 1

Guesses

	R	S	U	B	C	D
1.	—	—	—	—	—	—
2.	—	—	—	—	—	—
3.	—	—	—	—	—	—
4.	—	—	—	—	—	—

Graph:

GAME 2

Guesses

	R	S	U	B	C	D
1.	—	—	—	—	—	—
2.	—	—	—	—	—	—
3.	—	—	—	—	—	—
4.	—	—	—	—	—	—

Graph:

GAME 3

Guesses

	R	S	U	B	C	D
1.	—	—	—	—	—	—
2.	—	—	—	—	—	—
3.	—	—	—	—	—	—
4.	—	—	—	—	—	—

Graph:

EXERCISES

1. Which is the correct equation of the graph shown at the right?

   a. $y = (x - 2)(x - 0)(x - 4)$

   b. $y = (x + 2)(x - 0)(x - 4)$

   c. $y = (x - 2)(x - 0)(x + 4)$

   What are the x-intercepts of the graph.

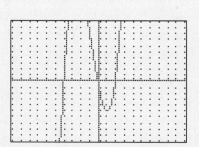

2. Write the equation of the graph shown in Exercise 1 in the form $y = x^3 + bx^2 + cx + d$.

*Problem Solving Using
a Graphing Calculator*

This demonstration and worksheet can be used for group instruction or by individual students with graphing calculators. On their worksheets, students are asked to describe a collection of data by constructing a bar graph of the data and by determining the mean, the standard deviation, and the range of the data.

EXAMPLE DESCRIBING A COLLECTION OF DATA

Fifteen students were asked how many hours each spent watching television on the previous Saturday. The responses were as follows.

4, 5, 0, 1, 4, 3, 2, 4, 7, 3, 4, 6, 7, 3, 1

a. Construct a bar graph for the data.

b. Determine the standard deviation of the data.

SOLUTION

a. To construct a bar graph of the data, follow the steps given on page 4 of this publication. Using the indicated range, you should obtain the display shown at the right.

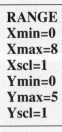

```
RANGE
Xmin=0
Xmax=8
Xscl=1
Ymin=0
Ymax=5
Yscl=1
```

b. To determine the standard deviation of the data, use the following steps. (The data has already been entered—in part **a.**)

TI-81: 2nd STAT 1 ENTER

CASIO fx-7700G: MODE × F4 F2 EXE

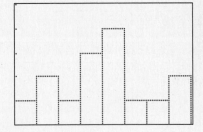

The Casio fx-7700G will display only the standard deviation for a population. The TI-81 will display the following.

$\bar{x} = 3.6000$ *Mean*

$\Sigma x = 54.0000$ *Sum of x-values*

$\Sigma x^2 = 256.0000$ *Sum of x²-values*

$S_x = 2.0976$ *Standard deviation for sample (uses "n − 1")*

$\sigma_x = 2.0264$ *Standard deviation for population (uses "n")*

$n = 15$ *Number of x-values in data*

In this display, note that two values for standard deviation are given. The first, S_x, is the "sample" standard deviation for the actual 15 data values. The second, σ_x, is the "population" standard deviation—when using a small sample to predict the standard deviation of a larger population, statisticians usually use S_x. The formulas used for the two standard deviations are as follows. (Notice the different denominators.)

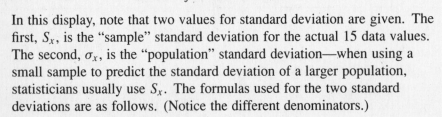

$$S_x = \sqrt{\frac{(x_1 - \bar{x})^2 + (x_2 - \bar{x})^2 + \cdots + (x_n - \bar{x})^2}{n - 1}}$$

$$\sigma_x = \sqrt{\frac{(x_1 - \bar{x})^2 + (x_2 - \bar{x})^2 + \cdots + (x_n - \bar{x})^2}{n}}$$

The *Algebra 2* text always uses the second formula—so the standard deviation of the data is 2.0264.

*Problem Solving Using
a Graphing Calculator*

On this worksheet, you are asked to calculate the standard deviation
of a collection of data by hand and then compare the result to that
given by a graphing calculator.

EXERCISES

In Exercises 1–4, use the following information.

Ten children were surveyed to determine the number of pets each had in
their homes. The results were 4, 1, 0, 1, 2, 3, 2, 4, 0, 3.

1. Find the range of the data. (Remember that the term range is used in
   different ways. In this context, it means the difference of the largest and
   smallest data values.)

2. Find the mean of the data. Then use a graphing calculator to verify your
   result.

3. Complete the following table. Then use the result to evaluate the standard
   deviation of the data by hand.

x_i	$x_i - \overline{x}$	$(x_i - \overline{x})^2$
4		
1		
0		
1		
2		
3		
2		
4		
0		
3		
Sums		

4. Use a graphing calculator to evaluate the standard deviation of the data.

9.7

Name _____

Problem Solving Using a Graphing Calculator

The bar graphs for some collections of data are "bell-shaped." For such collections, approximately 68% of the data lies within one standard deviation of the mean, approximately 95% of the data lies within two standard deviations of the mean, and nearly all of the data lies within three standard deviations of the mean.

Interval:	$(\bar{x} - s,\ \bar{x} + s)$	*About 68% of data*
Interval:	$(\bar{x} - 2s,\ \bar{x} + 2s)$	*About 95% of data*
Interval:	$(\bar{x} - 3s,\ \bar{x} + 3s)$	*About 100% of data*

In Exercises 5–8, use the following data.

4, 5, 0, 1, 4, 3, 2, 4, 3, 2, 4, 7, 3, 4, 6, 7, 3, 1

5. Use a graphing calculator to sketch a bar graph (or histogram) of the data. Copy the result in the blank screen below.

6. Use a graphing calculator to determine the mean and standard deviation of the data.

7. Use the results of Exercise 6 to write the following three intervals.

a. $(\bar{x} - s,\ \bar{x} + s)$ **b.** $(\bar{x} - 2s,\ \bar{x} + 2s)$ **c.** $(\bar{x} - 3s,\ \bar{x} + 3s)$

8. Complete the table to compare the actual percent of data that lies in each interval obtained in Exercise 7.

Interval	Numbers in Interval	Actual Percent of Data in Interval	Estimated Percent of Data in Interval
$(\bar{x} - s,\ \bar{x} + s)$			68%
$(\bar{x} - 2s,\ \bar{x} + 2s)$			95%
$(\bar{x} - 3s,\ \bar{x} + 3s)$			100%

10.4

Problem Solving Using a Graphing Calculator

This demonstration and worksheet can be used for group instruction or by individual students with graphing calculators. On their worksheets, students are asked to use a graphing calculator to solve rational equations.

EXAMPLE   SOLVING A RATIONAL EQUATION

Solve the equation. $\dfrac{7}{x+3} = \dfrac{x}{4}$

SOLUTION

Begin by sketching the graph of $y = \dfrac{7}{x+3} - \dfrac{x}{4}$.

Using the indicated range setting, you should obtain the graph shown below.

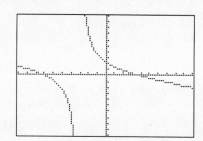

```
RANGE
Xmin=-10
Xmax=10
Xscl=1
Ymin=-10
Ymax=10
Yscl=1
```

By zooming in 2 or 3 times, you can see that the solutions are -7.0 and 4.0. Check these solutions algebraically by substituting in the original equation.

EXAMPLE   SOLVING A RATIONAL EQUATION

Solve the equation. $\dfrac{5x}{x-2} = 7 + \dfrac{10}{x-2}$

SOLUTION

Begin by sketching the graph of $y = 7 + \dfrac{10-5x}{x-2}$.

Using the indicated range setting, you should obtain the graph shown below.

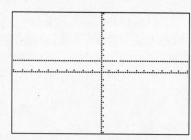

```
RANGE
Xmin=-10
Xmax=10
Xscl=1
Ymin=-10
Ymax=10
Yscl=1
```

From the display, you can see that the graph has no x-intercept, which implies that the equation has no solution. On the display, note that a "hole" appears at $x = 2$. This occurs because 2 is an extraneous solution.

10.4

Name _____

*Problem Solving Using
a Graphing Calculator*

On this worksheet, you are asked to use a graphing calculator to solve rational equations. After obtaining each solution, be sure to check it in the original equation.

EXERCISES

In Exercises 1–4, use a graphing calculator to solve the equation. In the blank screen provided, make a copy of the graph, showing *all* solutions.

1. $\dfrac{2x}{5} = \dfrac{x^2 - 5x}{5x}$

2. $\dfrac{2}{6x + 5} - \dfrac{3}{4(6x + 5)} = \dfrac{1}{28}$

3. $\dfrac{10}{x^2 - 2x} = \dfrac{3}{x^2 - 4} + 1$

4. $\dfrac{2x}{x + 2} = \dfrac{1}{x^2 - 4} + 1$

In Exercises 5–8, use a graphing calculator to solve the equation.

5. $\dfrac{x^2 - 4}{x^2 + 4x + 3} = 0$

6. $\dfrac{x + 2}{x - 2} = 0$

7. $\dfrac{2x}{4 - x} = \dfrac{x^2}{x - 4}$

8. $\dfrac{3x}{x + 1} = \dfrac{12}{x^2 - 1} + 2$

*Problem Solving
Using a Computer*

(See Exercises 5–8 on
page 558 of the text.)

This demonstration and worksheet can be used for group instruction
or by individual students with computers that have BASIC. On their
worksheets, students are asked to use a BASIC program to construct
an amortization table.

The objective of this demonstration and worksheet is to help students
understand how computers can be used in accounting.

BASIC PROGRAM

```
 10 PRINT "            BALANCE                                            BALANCE"
 20 PRINT "PAYMENT BEFORE                   INTEREST PRINCIPAL AFTER"
 30 PRINT "NUMBER  PAYMENT  PAYMENT PAYMENT PAYMENT PAYMENT"
 40 RAT=.105
 50 BAL=1200
 60 MON=9
 70 PAY=139.23
 80 FOR I=1 TO MON
 90 INS=BAL*RAT/12
100 INS=INT((INS+.005)*100)/100
110 IF I=MON THEN PAY=BAL+INS
120 PRI=PAY−INS
130 PRINT USING "#######";I;: PRINT "  ";
140 PRINT USING "$#,###.##";BAL;: PRINT "   ";
150 PRINT USING "$###.##";PAY;: PRINT "   ";
160 PRINT USING "$###.##";INS;: PRINT "   ";
170 PRINT USING "$###.##";PRI;: PRINT "   ";
180 BAL=BAL−PRI
190 PRINT USING "$#,###.##";BAL
200 NEXT
210 END
```

When this program is run, it will produce the amortization table for
Exercise 5 on page 558 of the text. For this program, a person has
borrowed $1200 at an annual interest rate of $10\frac{1}{2}\%$ to be repaid in nine
months. The first eight payments are $139.23 and the final payment is
$139.27. The printout for the program is as follows.

PAYMENT NUMBER	BALANCE BEFORE PAYMENT	PAYMENT	INTEREST PAYMENT	PRINCIPAL PAYMENT	BALANCE AFTER PAYMENT
1	$1200.00	$139.23	$10.50	$128.73	$1071.27
2	$1071.27	$139.23	$ 9.37	$129.86	$ 941.41
3	$ 941.41	$139.23	$ 8.24	$130.99	$ 810.42
4	$ 810.42	$139.23	$ 7.09	$132.14	$ 678.28
5	$ 678.28	$139.23	$ 5.93	$133.30	$ 544.98
6	$ 544.98	$139.23	$ 4.77	$134.46	$ 410.52
7	$ 410.52	$139.23	$ 3.59	$135.64	$ 274.88
8	$ 274.88	$139.23	$ 2.41	$136.82	$ 138.06
9	$ 138.06	$139.27	$ 1.21	$138.06	$ 0.00

10.6

Name _____

*Problem Solving
Using a Computer*

On this worksheet, you are asked to use a BASIC program to
construct an amortization table.

EXERCISES

1. You take out a loan for $560, at an annual interest rate of 8%, to be repaid
   in 9 monthly installments. What is the monthly payment?

2. Your teacher will give you a copy of a BASIC program that will construct
   an amortization table for a $1200 loan at $10\frac{1}{2}$% paid in monthly install-
   ments over a 9-month term. Alter the program so that it constructs an
   amortization table for the loan in Exercise 1.

3. After making the BASIC program changes requested in Exercise 2, run
   the program. Then copy the results in the spaces provided below.

PAYMENT NUMBER	BALANCE BEFORE PAYMENT	PAYMENT	INTEREST PAYMENT	PRINCIPAL PAYMENT	BALANCE AFTER PAYMENT
1					
2					
3					
4					
5					
6					
7					
8					
9					

4. Suppose you decided to repay the loan in 6 months. How would that
   change the BASIC program?

5. After making the BASIC program changes requested in Exercise 4, run
   the program. Then copy the results in the spaces provided below. How
   much interest would be saved by repaying the loan in 6 months instead of
   9 months?

PAYMENT NUMBER	BALANCE BEFORE PAYMENT	PAYMENT	INTEREST PAYMENT	PRINCIPAL PAYMENT	BALANCE AFTER PAYMENT
1					
2					
3					
4					
5					
6					

Problem Solving Using a Graphing Calculator

(See Exercises 9–12 on page 558 of the text.)

This demonstration and worksheet can be used for group instruction or by individual students with graphing calculators. On their worksheets, students are asked to use program **MORTGAGE** to find the monthly payment for a home mortgage.

The objective of this demonstration and worksheet is for students to decide whether a given mortgage fits a budget.

TI-81 Program

Prgm6: MORTGAGE
:Fix 2
:Disp "TOTAL MORTGAGE"
:Input P
:Disp "INTEREST RATE"
:Disp "IN DECIMAL FORM"
:Input R
:R/12→I
:Disp "NUMBER OF YEARS"
:Input T
:P(I/(1−(1/(1+I))∧(12T)))→M
:Disp "MONTHLY PAYMENT"
:Disp M
:Float

CASIO fx-7700G Program

MORTGAGE
Fix 2
"TOTAL MORTGAGE"
?→P
"INTEREST RATE"
"IN DECIMAL FORM"
?→R
R÷12→I
"NUMBER OF YEARS"
?→T
P(I÷(1−(1÷(1+I))x^y(12T)))→M
"MONTHLY PAYMENT"
M◢
Norm

EXAMPLE   FINDING A MORTGAGE PAYMENT

You have $30,000 for the down payment on a $145,000 house. Your bank will provide a 20-year mortgage at an 8.25% annual interest rate, compounded monthly. Your budget will not allow a monthly payment above $1000. Does this house fit your budget? If so, what is the total interest paid over the 20-year term?

SOLUTION

The total amount of the mortgage is as follows.

Mortgage	=	Cost of House	−	Down Payment

$$M = 145{,}000 - 30{,}000 = 115{,}000$$

```
TOTAL MORTGAGE
?115000
INTEREST RATE
IN DECIMAL FORM
?0.0825
NUMBER OF YEARS
?20
MONTHLY PAYMENT
            979.88
```

Thus, the total amount of the mortgage is $115,000. Use the program **MORTGAGE**. You should obtain the screen shown at the right. From the screen, you can see that the monthly payment is $979.88. This is within your monthly budget. The total amount of interest paid over the 20-year term is as follows.

Total Interest	=	Total Payments	−	Total Mortgage

$$T = 20(12)(979.88) - 115{,}000 = 120{,}171.20$$

Thus, the total interest paid is $120,171.20.

10.6   Name _____

*Problem Solving Using
a Graphing Calculator*

Program **MORTGAGE** allows you to use a graphing calculator to
calculate a monthly payment.

EXERCISES

In Exercises 1–4, determine the monthly payment for the home mortgage.
Then decide whether the home mortgage fits within the monthly mortgage
payment. Find the total interest paid over the term of the loan.

1. *List Price of House:* $79,500

   Down Payment: $35,000

   Total Mortgage: ☐

   Annual Interest Rate: 12.5%

   Term of Mortgage: 15 years

   Monthly Payment: ☐

   Total Interest: ☐

   Monthly Budget: $1050

   Fits Budget?   ☐

2. *List Price of House:* $143,260

   Down Payment: $35,000

   Total Mortgage: ☐

   Annual Interest Rate: 12.5%

   Term of Mortgage: 20 years

   Monthly Payment: ☐

   Total Interest: ☐

   Monthly Budget: $1050

   Fits Budget?   ☐

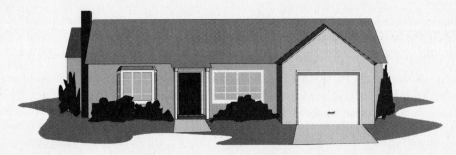

3. *List Price of House:* $158,500

   Down Payment: $35,000

   Total Mortgage: ☐

   Annual Interest Rate: 8.2%

   Term of Mortgage: 20 years

   Monthly Payment: ☐

   Total Interest: ☐

   Monthly Budget: $1050

   Fits Budget?   ☐

4. *List Price of House:* $158,500

   Down Payment: $35,000

   Total Mortgage: ☐

   Annual Interest Rate: 9.2%

   Term of Mortgage: 20 years

   Monthly Payment: ☐

   Total Interest: ☐

   Monthly Budget: $1050

   Fits Budget?   ☐

*Problem Solving Using
a Graphing Calculator*

(See Exercises 17–28 on
page 579 of the text.)

This demonstration and worksheet can be used for group instruction or by individual students with graphing calculators. On their worksheets, students are asked to use a graphing calculator to sketch the graph of a circle whose center is the origin.

The objective of this demonstration and worksheet is for students to realize that graphs of circles cannot be expressed as a single function of x.

EXAMPLE SKETCHING CIRCLES IN TWO PARTS

Use a graphing calculator to sketch the circle given by

$$x^2 + y^2 = 16.$$

Then determine the radius, the x-intercepts, and the y-intercepts of the circle.

SOLUTION

Begin by solving the equation for y.

$x^2 + y^2 = 16$	*Equation of circle*
$y^2 = 16 - x^2$	*Subtract x^2 from both sides.*
$y = \pm\sqrt{16 - x^2}$	*Take square root of both sides.*

The circle cannot be represented by a single function of x. It can, however, be represented by two functions of x.

$y = \sqrt{16 - x^2}$	*Top half of circle*
$y = -\sqrt{16 - x^2}$	*Bottom half of circle*

To sketch the graph of the circle, graph both functions on the same screen as shown below. From the graph, you can see that the radius is 4. The x-intercepts are (-4, 0) and (4, 0). The y-intercepts are (0, -4) and (0, 4).

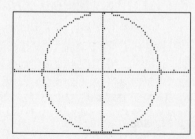

RANGE
Xmin=-6
Xmax=6
Xscl=1
Ymin=-4
Ymax=4
Yscl=1

When graphing circles on a graphing calculator (or any other graphing utility), be sure to use a "square setting" in which the tic-spacing is the same on both axes.

11.2

Name _____

Problem Solving Using a Graphing Calculator

On this worksheet, you are asked to use a graphing calculator to sketch circles. As a reference, you should read the graphing calculator feature on page 604 of the text.

EXERCISES

In Exercises 1–4, consider the equation $x^2 + y^2 = 25$.

1. When you solve this equation for y, you obtain two functions of x. What are they? Which parts of the circle do these functions represent?

2. Why can't the graph of the circle be represented by a single function of x?

3. What is the radius of the circle? What are the x- and y-intercepts?

4. Use a graphing calculator to sketch both parts of the circle on the same screen. Which range produces a graph that appears circular? Explain why the second range is called a "square" setting?

RANGE
Xmin=-6
Xmax=6
Xscl=1
Ymin=-6
Ymax=6
Yscl=1

RANGE
Xmin=-9
Xmax=9
Xscl=1
Ymin=-6
Ymax=6
Yscl=1

5. Sketch the graph of equation. Use an appropriate square setting so that the graph appears circular. Copy your results in the spaces below.

$x^2 + y^2 = 100$ $x^2 + y^2 = 144$ $x^2 + y^2 = 225$

In 6–8, find the points of intersection algebraically *and* graphically.

6. $x^2 + y^2 = 676$
   $x + y = 34$

7. $x^2 + y^2 = 100$
   $2x + 2y = 28$

8. $x^2 + y^2 = 16$
   $y + 4 = 0$

Problem Solving Using a Graphing Calculator

(See Exercises 29–40 on page 587 of the text.)

This demonstration and worksheet can be used for group instruction or by individual students with graphing calculators. On their worksheets, students are asked to use a graphing calculator to sketch the graph of an ellipse whose center is the origin.

The objective of this demonstration and worksheet is for students to understand the concept of eccentricity. The eccentricity of an ellipse

$$\frac{x^2}{a^2} + \frac{y^2}{b^2} = 1 \quad \text{or} \quad \frac{x^2}{b^2} + \frac{y^2}{a^2} = 1$$

is $\frac{c}{a}$ where $c = \sqrt{a^2 - b^2}$. The eccentricity, e, of an ellipse is a number such that $0 < e < 1$. If e is close to zero, then the ellipse is nearly circular. If e is close to 1, then the ellipse is elongated.

EXAMPLE   COMPARING ECCENTRICITIES OF ELLIPSES

Use a graphing calculator to sketch the ellipses. (Use a square setting.) Then calculate the eccentricity of each ellipse.

a. $\dfrac{x^2}{10.1^2} + \dfrac{y^2}{10^2} = 1$ **b.** $\dfrac{x^2}{36^2} + \dfrac{y^2}{10^2} = 1$

SOLUTION

a. For this ellipse, $a = 10.1$, $b = 10$, and

$$c = \sqrt{(10.1)^2 - 10^2} = \sqrt{2.01} \approx 1.4.$$

Thus, the eccentricity is $e \approx \frac{c}{a} \approx 0.14$. This ellipse is nearly circular.

RANGE
Xmin=-15
Xmax=15
Xscl=1
Ymin=-10
Ymax=10
Yscl=1

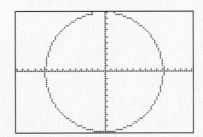

b. For this ellipse, $a = 36$, $b = 10$, and

$$c = \sqrt{36^2 - 10^2} = \sqrt{1196} \approx 34.6.$$

Thus, the eccentricity is $e \approx \frac{c}{a} \approx 0.96$. This ellipse is quite elongated.

RANGE
Xmin=-36
Xmax=36
Xscl=3
Ymin=-24
Ymax=24
Yscl=3

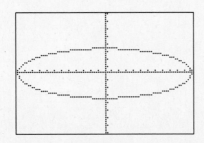

*Problem Solving Using
a Graphing Calculator*

On this worksheet, you are asked to use a graphing calculator
to sketch the graph of an ellipse and find its eccentricity. As a
reference, you should read the graphing calculator feature on page
604 of the text.

EXERCISES

1. Sketch the graph of equation. (Use a square setting.) Find the eccentricity
   of each ellipse. Which ellipse is most nearly circular? Which is most
   elongated?

$$\frac{x^2}{6^2} + \frac{y^2}{7^2} = 1$$
   $$\frac{x^2}{6^2} + \frac{y^2}{9^2} = 1$$
   $$\frac{x^2}{6^2} + \frac{y^2}{24^2} = 1$$

2. Use a graphing calculator to sketch the graph of

   $$\frac{x^4}{6^4} + \frac{y^4}{4^4} = 1.$$

   Copy the results in the blank screen below.

RANGE
Xmin=-9
Xmax=9
Xscl=1
Ymin=-6
Ymax=6
Yscl=1

3. In ordinary English, the terms *oval* and *elliptical* are synonyms. In
   mathematics, however, the terms are not synonyms. Is the graph of the
   equation in Exercise 2 an ellipse? Is the graph of the equation in Exercise
   2 an oval?

Problem Solving Using a Graphing Calculator

(See Exercises 23–38 on page 602 of the text.)

This demonstration and worksheet can be used for group instruction or by individual students with graphing calculators. On their worksheets, students are asked to use a graphing calculator to sketch the graph of a conic whose center has been translated (from the origin).

The objective of this demonstration and worksheet is for students to understand the concept of horizontal and vertical shifts of graphs.

EXAMPLE TRANSLATING CONICS

Use a graphing calculator to sketch the conic. (Use a square setting.)

a. $(x - 2)^2 + y^2 = 16$

b. $\dfrac{(x - 1)^2}{4^2} + \dfrac{(y + 2)^2}{3^2} = 1$

c. $\dfrac{(y - 1)^2}{4^2} - \dfrac{(x + 2)^2}{3^2} = 1$

SOLUTION

a. This graph is a circle whose center is (2, 0) and whose radius is 4. To sketch the circle on a graphing calculator, solve the equation for y. You will obtain two equations

$$y = \sqrt{16 - (x - 2)^2}$$
$$y = -\sqrt{16 - (x - 2)^2}$$

which represent the top and bottom halves of the circle.

b. This graph is an ellipse whose center is (1, -2). The length of the major axis is $2a = 8$ and the length of the minor axis is $2b = 6$. Solving the equation for y produces two equations

$$y = 3\sqrt{1 - \tfrac{1}{16}(x - 1)^2} - 2$$
$$y = -3\sqrt{1 - \tfrac{1}{16}(x - 1)^2} - 2$$

which represent the top and bottom halves of the ellipse.

c. This graph is a hyperbola whose center is (-2, 1). To sketch the hyperbola on a graphing calculator, solve the equation for y. You will obtain two equations

$$y = 4\sqrt{1 + \tfrac{1}{9}(x + 2)^2} + 1$$
$$y = -4\sqrt{1 + \tfrac{1}{9}(x + 2)^2} + 1$$

which represent the two branches of the hyperbola.

```
RANGE
Xmin=-5
Xmax=7
Xscl=1
Ymin=-4
Ymax=4
Yscl=1
```

```
RANGE
Xmin=-5
Xmax=7
Xscl=1
Ymin=-6
Ymax=2
Yscl=1
```

```
RANGE
Xmin=-16
Xmax=14
Xscl=1
Ymin=-9
Ymax=11
Yscl=1
```

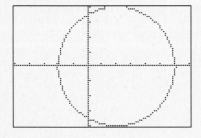

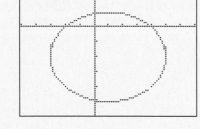

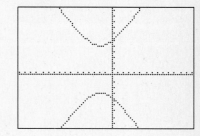

Problem Solving Using a Graphing Calculator

On this worksheet, you are asked to use a graphing calculator to sketch the graph of a conic whose center has been translated away from the origin.

EXERCISES

1. Use a graphing calculator to sketch the graph of the equation. (Use a square setting.) Classify the conic as a circle, an ellipse, or a hyperbola. Find the coordinates of the center of the conic.

$$\frac{(x-2)^2}{4^2} + \frac{(y-2)^2}{4^2} = 1$$

Center: _____

Conic: _____

$$\frac{(x-2)^2}{4^2} - \frac{(y-2)^2}{3^2} = 1$$

Center: _____

Conic: _____

$$\frac{(x-2)^2}{3^2} + \frac{(y-2)^2}{4^2} = 1$$

Center: _____

Conic: _____

2. Use a graphing calculator to sketch the graph of the equation. (Use a square setting.) Classify the conic as a circle, an ellipse, or a hyperbola. Find the coordinates of the center of the conic.

$$\frac{(y+2)^2}{2^2} - \frac{(x-3)^2}{2^2} = 1$$

Center: _____

Conic: _____

$$\frac{(y+2)^2}{2^2} + \frac{(x-3)^2}{3^2} = 1$$

Center: _____

Conic: _____

$$\frac{(y+2)^2}{3^2} + \frac{(x-3)^2}{2^2} = 1$$

Center: _____

Conic: _____

Exploration Using a Graphing Calculator

(See Exercises 13–28 on page 648 of the text.)

This demonstration and worksheet can be used for group instruction or by individual students with graphing calculators. On their worksheets, students are asked to sketch the first *n* partial sums of the series. Based on the sketch, students are asked to decide whether the series has a sum.

The program **G.SERIES** is a teacher demonstration program that prompts the user to input *positive A* (the first term of the sequence) and *R* (the common ratio of the sequence). The program then produces a graph of (up to) the first 20 partial sums.

The first two worksheets should be given to students to complete *during* the teacher demonstration.

TI-81 PROGRAM

```
Prgm1:G.SERIES
:Grid Off
:All-Off
:ClrDraw
:Disp "POSITIVE A?"
:Input A
:Disp "R?"
:Input R
:-5→Xmin
:20→Xmax
:1→Xscl
:-5→Ymin
:2A→Ymax
:If R>1
:Goto 3
:Goto 4
:Lbl 3
:(A−AR∧20)/(1−R)→Ymax
:-Ymax→Ymin
:Goto 2
:Lbl 4
:If R=1
:Goto 5
:Goto 6
:Lbl 5
:20A→Ymax
:-.1Ymax→Ymin
:Goto 2
:Lbl 6
:If (0<R)(R<1)=1
:Goto 7
```

```
:Goto 8
:Lbl 7
:(A/(1−R))+A→Ymax
:-.1Ymax→Ymin
:Goto 2
:Lbl 8
:If R=0
:Goto 2
:If (-1<R)(R<0)=1
:Goto 9
:Goto A
:Lbl 9
:A→Ymax
:A+RA→Ymin
:Goto 2
:Lbl A
:If R=-1
:Goto B
:Goto C
:Lbl B
:1.2A→Ymax
:-.1Ymax→Ymin
:Goto 2
:Lbl C
:If R<-1
:Goto D
:Goto 2
:Lbl D
:-(A−AR∧20)/(1−R)→Ymax
:-Ymax→Ymin
:Lbl 2
```

```
:Ymax−Ymin→Y
:Y/10→H
:Int(logH)→Y
:10∧Y→Y
:IPart(.5+H/Y)→H
:HY→Yscl
:Disp "Yscl"
:Disp Yscl
:1→N
:A→S
:Pause
:Lbl 1
:Disp "N="
:Disp N
:Disp "S(N)"
:Disp S
:Pause
:PT-On (N,S)
:Pause
:AR∧N+S→S
:N+1→N
:If N≤20
:Goto 1
:Disp "Yscl="
:Disp Yscl
:If abs R≥1
:End
:A/(1−R)→X
:Pause
:Disp "S(INFINITE N)="
:Disp X
```

12.4

Name _____

*Exploration Using a
Graphing Calculator*

On this worksheet, you are asked to use the program **G.SERIES** to
determine whether an infinite geometric series has a sum.

EXERCISES

1. First term:

$a_1 = 120$

Common ratio:

$r = 1.2$

*First 5 terms of
geometric sequence:*

*First 5 partial sums
of geometric series:*

Graph of partial sums:

Conclusion:

☐ Series has a sum.

☐ Series has no sum.

Sum of the series:

Yscl:

---

2. First term:

$a_1 = 65$

Common ratio:

$r = 1$

*First 5 terms of
geometric sequence:*

*First 5 partial sums
of geometric series:*

Graph of partial sums:

Conclusion:

☐ Series has a sum.

☐ Series has no sum.

Sum of the series:

Yscl:

---

3. First term:

$a_1 = 5000$

Common ratio:

$r = 0.8$

*First 5 terms of
geometric sequence:*

*First 5 partial sums
of geometric series:*

Graph of partial sums:

Conclusion:

☐ Series has a sum.

☐ Series has no sum.

Sum of the series:

Yscl:

---

4. First term:

$a_1 = 50$

Common ratio:

$r = 0.5$

*First 5 terms of
geometric sequence:*

*First 5 partial sums
of geometric series:*

Graph of partial sums:

Conclusion:

☐ Series has a sum.

☐ Series has no sum.

Sum of the series:

Yscl:

---

5. First term:

$a_1 = 100$

Common ratio:

$r = 0$

*First 5 terms of
geometric sequence*:

*First 5 partial sums
of geometric series*:

Graph of partial sums:

Conclusion:

☐ Series has a sum.

☐ Series has no sum.

Sum of the series:

Yscl:

6. First term:

$a_1 = 8$

Common ratio:

$r = -0.6$

*First 5 terms of
geometric sequence*:

*First 5 partial sums
of geometric series*:

Graph of partial sums:

Conclusion:

☐ Series has a sum.

☐ Series has no sum.

Sum of the series:

Yscl:

7. First term:

$a_1 = 100$

Common ratio:

$r = -0.95$

*First 5 terms of
geometric sequence*:

*First 5 partial sums
of geometric series*:

Graph of partial sums:

Conclusion:

☐ Series has a sum.

☐ Series has no sum.

Sum of the series:

Yscl:

8. First term:

$a_1 = 400$

Common ratio:

$r = -1$

*First 5 terms of
geometric sequence*:

*First 5 partial sums
of geometric series*:

Graph of partial sums:

Conclusion:

☐ Series has a sum.

☐ Series has no sum.

Sum of the series:

Yscl:

*Exploration Using a
Graphing Calculator*

On this worksheet, you are asked to use the program **G.SERIES** to
determine whether an infinite geometric series has a sum.

EXERCISES

In Exercises 1–7, choose a positive first term for a geometric series, and
choose a common ratio with the given restriction. Then, run the program
G.SERIES and decide whether the infinite geometric series has a sum.

First Term	Restriction	Common Ratio	Sum of Infinite Series
1. $a_1 = $ _____	$r > 1$	$r = $ _____	Sum = _____
2. $a_1 = $ _____	$r = 1$	$r = $ _____	Sum = _____
3. $a_1 = $ _____	$0 < r < 1$	$r = $ _____	Sum = _____
4. $a_1 = $ _____	$r = 0$	$r = $ _____	Sum = _____
5. $a_1 = $ _____	$-1 < r < 0$	$r = $ _____	Sum = _____
6. $a_1 = $ _____	$r = -1$	$r = $ _____	Sum = _____
7. $a_1 = $ _____	$r < -1$	$r = $ _____	Sum = _____

8. What conclusions can you make from the results of Exercises 1–7? Does
the value of a_1 effect whether an infinite geometric series has a sum?
Does the value of r effect whether an infinite geometric series has a sum?
Explain.

Problem Solving Using a Graphing Calculator

(See Exercises 7–36 on page 655 of the text.)

This demonstration and worksheet can be used for group instruction or by individual students with graphing calculators. On their worksheets, students are asked to use a graphing calculator to compute binomial coefficients.

The objectives of this demonstration and worksheet are to acquaint students with the probability menus of a graphing calculator *and* to reinforce the formula for binomial coefficients.

EXAMPLE COMPUTING BINOMIAL COEFFICIENTS

Compute the fourth row of Pascal's Triangle by hand. Then verify your results with a graphing calculator.

SOLUTION

Begin by computing the binomial coefficients by hand.

$$\binom{4}{0} = \frac{4!}{4!0!} = \frac{4 \cdot 3 \cdot 2 \cdot 1}{4 \cdot 3 \cdot 2 \cdot 1 \cdot 1} = 1$$

$$\binom{4}{1} = \frac{4!}{3!1!} = \frac{4 \cdot 3 \cdot 2 \cdot 1}{3 \cdot 2 \cdot 1 \cdot 1} = 4$$

$$\binom{4}{2} = \frac{4!}{2!2!} = \frac{4 \cdot 3 \cdot 2 \cdot 1}{2 \cdot 1 \cdot 2 \cdot 1} = 6$$

$$\binom{4}{3} = \frac{4!}{1!3!} = \frac{4 \cdot 3 \cdot 2 \cdot 1}{1 \cdot 3 \cdot 2 \cdot 1} = 4$$

$$\binom{4}{4} = \frac{4!}{0!4!} = \frac{4 \cdot 3 \cdot 2 \cdot 1}{1 \cdot 4 \cdot 3 \cdot 2 \cdot 1} = 1$$

Thus, the fourth row of Pascal's Triangle is as follows.

1   4   6   4   1

To verify these results on a graphing calculator, use the following keystrokes. On the Casio fx-7700G, make sure you are not in BASE-N Mode.

TI-81: 4 MATH ◁ 3 0 ENTER
Display: 1
4 MATH ◁ 3 1 ENTER
Display: 4
4 MATH ◁ 3 2 ENTER
Display: 6
4 MATH ◁ 3 3 ENTER
Display: 4
4 MATH ◁ 3 4 ENTER
Display: 1

CASIO fx-7700G: 4 SHIFT MATH F2 F3 0 EXE
Display: 1
4 SHIFT MATH F2 F3 1 EXE
Display: 4
4 SHIFT MATH F2 F3 2 EXE
Display: 6
4 SHIFT MATH F2 F3 3 EXE
Display: 4
4 SHIFT MATH F2 F3 4 EXE
Display: 1

12.5

Name _____

Problem Solving Using a Graphing Calculator

On this worksheet, you are asked to use a graphing calculator to compute and use binomial coefficients. For example, to compute the binomial coefficient $\binom{6}{2}$, you can use the following keystrokes.

TI-81:   6 $\boxed{\text{MATH}}$ $\boxed{\triangleleft}$ $\boxed{3}$ 2 $\boxed{\text{ENTER}}$ *Display: 15*

CASIO fx-7700G: 6 $\boxed{\text{SHIFT}}$ $\boxed{\text{MATH}}$ $\boxed{\text{F2}}$ $\boxed{\text{F3}}$ 2 $\boxed{\text{EXE}}$ *Display: 15*

You can verify this result by hand calculations.

$$\binom{6}{2} = \frac{6!}{4!2!} = \frac{6 \cdot 5 \cdot 4 \cdot 3 \cdot 2 \cdot 1}{4 \cdot 3 \cdot 2 \cdot 1 \cdot 2 \cdot 1} = 15$$

EXERCISES

1. Use a graphing calculator to derive the ninth row of Pascal's Triangle.

$$\binom{9}{0} \quad \binom{9}{1} \quad \binom{9}{2} \quad \binom{9}{3} \quad \binom{9}{4} \quad \binom{9}{5} \quad \binom{9}{6} \quad \binom{9}{7} \quad \binom{9}{8} \quad \binom{9}{9}$$

___   ___   ___   ___   ___   ___   ___   ___   ___   ___

2. Write the variable part for each term in the expansion of $(x + y)^9$.

$\underline{x^9 y^0}$ $\underline{x^8 y^1}$ ___   ___   ___   ___   ___   ___   ___   ___

3. Use the results of Exercises 1 and 2 to write the complete expansion of $(x + y)^9$.

$(x + y)^9 =$ _____

4. Use a graphing calculator to derive the seventh row of Pascal's Triangle.

$$\binom{7}{0} \quad \binom{7}{1} \quad \binom{7}{2} \quad \binom{7}{3} \quad \binom{7}{4} \quad \binom{7}{5} \quad \binom{7}{6} \quad \binom{7}{7}$$

___   ___   ___   ___   ___   ___   ___   ___

5. Complete the following parts of the expansion of $(2x + 1)^7$.

$\underline{(2x)^7(1)^0}$ $\underline{(2x)^6(1)^1}$ ____   ____   ____   ____   ____   ____

6. Use the results of Exercises 4 and 5 to write the complete expansion of $(2x + 1)^7$.

$(2x + 1)^7 =$ _____

In Exercise 7–9, use a graphing calculator to compute the binomial coefficient.

7. $\binom{12}{7}$ 8. $\binom{14}{8}$ 9. $\binom{16}{6}$

12.6

Problem Solving Using a Spreadsheet

(See Exercises 7–10 on
page 661 of the text.)

This demonstration and worksheet can be used for group instruction or by individual students with spreadsheet software. On their worksheets, students are asked to use a spreadsheet to construct an annuity table.

The objectives of this demonstration and worksheet are for students to learn how to create a spreadsheet and how to use a spreadsheet to perform repeated calculations.

EXAMPLE   CONSTRUCTING AN ANNUITY TABLE

You deposit $1000 in an annuity at the end of each year for 6 years. The annuity pays 6%, compounded annually. Construct an annuity table that shows the balances after the first six deposits.

SOLUTION

	A	B	C	D	E
1	1	$0.00	$0.00	$1,000.00	$1,000.00
2	2	$1,000.00	$60.00	$1,000.00	$2,060.00
3	3	$2,060.00	$123.60	$1,000.00	$3,183.60
4	4	$3,183.60	$191.02	$1,000.00	$4,374.62
5	5	$4,374.62	$262.48	$1,000.00	$5,637.10
6	6	$5,637.10	$338.23	$1,000.00	$6,975.33

Column	Description of Data	Data Type	Sample Formula
Column A	This column contains the year number. These numbers should be entered one at a time—they are part of the *input data*.	Input	—
Column B	This column contains the previous balance. Note that B1 is 0, but B2 through B6 correspond to the values of the new balances in locations E1 through E5. This means that you should enter the formula "E1" in location B2. This formula can then be copied to the other locations in column B. As it copies, the computer will make appropriate changes in the formula. For instance, the formula "E2" will be copied to location B3.	Output	E1
Column C	This column contains the interest, computed on an annual basis. This column should be entered as a formula. Enter the formula "B1∗0.06" in location C1. Then copy the formula to the other locations in column C.	Output	B1∗0.06
Column D	This column is the deposit for each year. It should be entered as $1000 in location D1 and then copied to the other locations in column D.	Input	1000
Column E	This column is the new balance for the end of each year. The formula "B1+C1+D1" should be entered in location E1, and then copied to the other locations in column E.	Output	B1+C1+D1

12.6   Name _____

*Problem Solving
Using a Spreadsheet*

On this worksheet, you are asked to use a spreadsheet to construct an
annuity table.

EXERCISES

1. Your mother decides to create an annuity for your college education.
   Beginning on your 1st birthday, she deposit $1000 at the end of each
   year for 18 years. The annuity pays 5.5%, compounded annually. Use a
   spreadsheet to complete the following annuity table.

	End of Year	Previous Balance	Interest	Deposit	New Balance
	A	B	C	D	E
1	1	0.00	0.00	$1,000.00	$1,000.00
2	2	$1,000.00	$55.00	$1,000.00	
3	3			$1,000.00	
4	4			$1,000.00	
5	5			$1,000.00	
6	6			$1,000.00	
7	7			$1,000.00	
8	8			$1,000.00	
9	9			$1,000.00	
10	10			$1,000.00	
11	11			$1,000.00	
12	12			$1,000.00	
13	13			$1,000.00	
14	14			$1,000.00	
15	15			$1,000.00	
16	16			$1,000.00	
17	17			$1,000.00	
18	18			$1,000.00	

2. What is the total interest earned in the annuity in Exercise 1?

3. How much more interest would be earned if the annuity paid 7%,
   compounded annually, instead of 5.5%?

Exploration Using a Graphing Calculator

(See Exercises 55–62 on page 690 of the text.)

This demonstration and worksheet can be used for group instruction or by individual students with graphing calculators. On their worksheets, students are asked to use a graphing calculator to sketch the unit circle and to sketch angles in standard position.

The objective of this demonstration and worksheet is to help build students intuition for the radian and degree measure of angles.

TI-81 PROGRAM

Prgm:ANGLE
:Lbl 1
:Disp "ENTER MODE"
:Disp "0=RADIAN"
:Disp "1=DEGREE"
:Input M
:Disp "ENTER ANGLE"
:Input T
:If M=1
:πT/180→T
:Rad
:ClrDraw
:All-Off
:-1.5→Xmin
:1.5→Xmax
:1→Xscl
:-1→Ymin
:1→Ymax

:1→Yscl
:0→Tmin
:abs T→Tmax
:.15→Tstep
:cos T→A
:sin T→B
:Param
:1→S
:If T<0
:-1→S
:"(.25+0.04T)cos T"→X_{1T}
:"S(.25+0.04T)sin T"→Y_{1T}
:DispGraph
:Line(0,0,A,B)
:Pause
:Function
:All-On
:Goto 1

When program **ANGLE** is run, it prompts the user to choose between radian and degree mode. It then prompts the user to enter an angle. After entering the angle measure and pressing ENTER or EXE, the calculator will sketch the angle in standard position. Two examples are shown below.

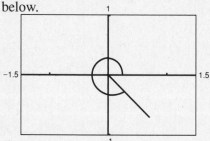

Radian Measure: $\theta = \frac{7\pi}{4}$

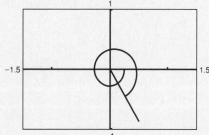

Degree Measure: $\theta = -420°$

13.2   Name _____

Exploration Using a Graphing Calculator

On this worksheet, you are asked to use the graphing calculator program **ANGLE** to sketch angles. When the program is run, you should enter 0 for radian mode or 1 for degree mode. Then press $\boxed{\text{ENTER}}$ or $\boxed{\text{EXE}}$. Next, enter the measure of the angle you want to draw, followed by $\boxed{\text{ENTER}}$ or $\boxed{\text{EXE}}$.

EXERCISES

In Exercises 1–6, use the program **ANGLE** to sketch the angle. Copy the results in the blank screen.

1. Radians: $\theta = \frac{2\pi}{3}$

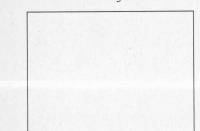

2. Radians: $\theta = \frac{11\pi}{3}$

3. Radians: $\theta = -\frac{5\pi}{4}$

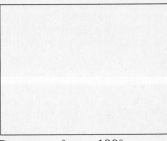

4. Degrees: $\theta = 75°$

5. Degrees: $\theta = 420°$

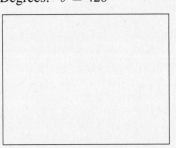

6. Degrees: $\theta = -190°$

In Exercise 7–9, use the program **ANGLE** to estimate the radian measure and degree measure of the angle.

7.

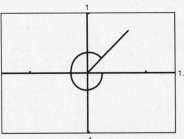

8.

9.

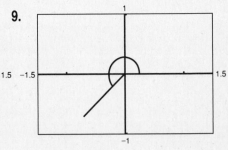

Exploration Using a Graphing Calculator

This demonstration and worksheet can be used for group instruction or by individual students with graphing calculators. On their worksheets, students are asked to use a graphing calculator to sketch the unit circle, an angle, and then estimate the sine and cosine of the angle.

The objective of this demonstration and worksheet is to help students understand the "unit circle" definition of the sine and cosine functions.

EXAMPLE   ESTIMATING TRIGONOMETRIC FUNCTIONS

Begin by setting the calculator to parametric and degree modes.

TI-81: [MODE], cursor to **DEG**, [ENTER], cursor to **PARAM**, [ENTER]

CASIO fx-7700G: [SHIFT] [DRG] [F1] [EXE] [MODE] [SHIFT] [×]

Next, set the range.

Tmin = 0	Xmin=-1.5	Ymin=-1
Tmax = 360	Xmax=1.5	Ymax=1
Tstep = 1	Xscl=1	Yscl=1

Finally, enter the sine and cosine functions in parametric mode.

TI-81: [Y=] [cos] [X|T] [ENTER] [sin] [X|T] [ENTER] [GRAPH]

CASIO fx-7700G: [Graph] [cos] [X,θ,T] [SHIFT] [,] [sin] [X,θ,T] [)] [EXE]

The calculator will display the unit circle as shown below. By using the trace key, you can move the cursor around the unit circle. The displayed value of T is the measure of θ in degrees. The displayed value of X is the cosine of θ and the displayed value of Y is the sine of θ.

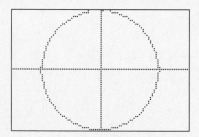

For example, the point on the unit circle that corresponds to $\theta = 120°$ is (-0.5, 0.8660254), which implies that

$$\cos 120° = -0.5 \quad \text{and} \quad \sin 120° \approx 0.8660254.$$

13.3

Name _____

Exploration Using a Graphing Calculator

On this worksheet, you are asked to use a graphing calculator to estimate the sine and cosine of an angle.

EXERCISES

In Exercise 1–12, use a graphing calculator to estimate the sine and cosine of the angle. Use the following steps.

a. Set the calculator to degree mode.

   TI-81: MODE , cursor to **DEG**, ENTER

   CASIO fx-7700G: SHIFT DRG F1 EXE

b. Set the calculator to parametric mode.

   TI-81: MODE , cursor to **PARAM**, ENTER

   CASIO fx-7700G: MODE SHIFT ×

c. Set the range.

Tmin = 0	Xmin=-1.5	Ymin=-1
Tmax = 360	Xmax=1.5	Ymax=1
Tstep = 1	Xscl=1	Yscl=1

d. Sketch the unit circle in parametric mode.

   TI-81: Y= cos X|T ENTER sin X|T ENTER GRAPH

   CASIO fx-7700G: Graph cos X,θ,T SHIFT , sin X,θ,T) EXE

   The calculator will display the unit circle. By using the trace key, you can move the cursor around the unit circle. The displayed value of T is the measure of θ in degrees. The displayed value of X is the cosine of θ and the displayed value of Y is the sine of θ.

1. 10°   **2.** 30°   **3.** 45°

4. 60°   **5.** 90°   **6.** 120°

7. 190°   **8.** 200°   **9.** 245°

10. 246°   **11.** 300°   **12.** 350°

13. Use the results of this activity to explain why $\sin\theta$ is positive in Quadrants I and II and negative in Quadrants III and IV.

14. Use the results of this activity to explain why $\cos\theta$ is positive in Quadrants I and IV and negative in Quadrants II and III.

14.1

*Problem Solving Using
a Graphing Calculator*

This demonstration and worksheet can be used for group instruction or by individual students with graphing calculators. On their worksheets, students are asked to classify sine waves by amplitude and frequency.

The objective of this demonstration and worksheet is to help students understand how changes in *a* and *b* affect the amplitude and frequency of the graph of $y = a \sin bx$.

EXAMPLE FINDING AMPLITUDES, PERIODS, AND FREQUENCIES

Use a graphing calculator to sketch the graphs of the following sine functions. Use the graph to determine the amplitude, period, and frequency of the graph. Be sure your calculator is in radian mode.

a. $y = 2 \sin x$

b. $y = 3 \sin 2x$

c. $y = 4 \sin 4x$

SOLUTION

a. The graph of this sine wave oscillates between $y = -2$ and $y = 2$. Thus, the graph has an amplitude of 2. Because the graph completes one cycle in the interval $0 \le x \le 2\pi$, it has a period of 2π. This implies that it has a frequency of $\frac{1}{2\pi}$.

b. The graph of this sine wave oscillates between $y = -3$ and $y = 3$. Thus, the graph has an amplitude of 3. Because the graph completes one cycle in the interval $0 \le x \le \pi$, it has a period of π. This implies that it has a frequency of $\frac{1}{\pi}$.

c. The graph of this sine wave oscillates between $y = -4$ and $y = 4$. Thus, the graph has an amplitude of 4. Because the graph completes one cycle in the interval $0 \le x \le \frac{\pi}{2}$, it has a period of $\frac{\pi}{2}$. This implies that it has a frequency of $\frac{2}{\pi}$.

```
RANGE
Xmin=-6.28
Xmax=6.28
Xscl=1.57
Ymin=-4
Ymax=4
Yscl=1
```

```
RANGE
Xmin=-6.28
Xmax=6.28
Xscl=1.57
Ymin=-4
Ymax=4
Yscl=1
```

```
RANGE
Xmin=-6.28
Xmax=6.28
Xscl=1.57
Ymin=-4
Ymax=4
Yscl=1
```

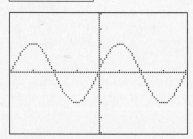

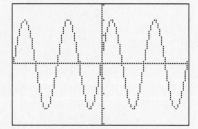

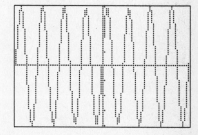

Radio waves can be modeled by sine waves. AM (amplitude modulation) radio waves alter the amplitude of the radio wave to send different signals. FM (frequency modulation) radio waves alter the frequency of the radio wave to send different signals.

14.1

Name _____

Problem Solving Using
a Graphing Calculator

On this worksheet, you are asked to use a graphing calculator to sketch the graph of sine waves. The amplitude of the graph of $y = a \sin bx$ is $|a|$. The period is $\frac{2\pi}{|b|}$, and the frequency is the reciprocal of the period.

Radio waves can be modeled by sine waves. AM (amplitude modulation) radio waves alter the amplitude of the radio wave to send different signals. FM (frequency modulation) radio waves alter the frequency of the radio wave to send different signals.

EXERCISES

In Exercises 1–3, use a graphing calculator to sketch the graph of the sine wave. Then determine the amplitude, period, and frequency of the sine wave. Before sketching the graph, be sure to set the calculator to radian mode.

Sine Wave	Characteristics	Range	Graph

1. $y = 3 \sin 2x$

Amplitude:

Period:

Frequency:

RANGE
Xmin=-6.28
Xmax=6.28
Xscl=1.57
Ymin=-4
Ymax=4
Yscl=1

2. $y = 2 \sin \frac{1}{2}x$

Amplitude:

Period:

Frequency:

RANGE
Xmin=-6.28
Xmax=6.28
Xscl=1.57
Ymin=-4
Ymax=4
Yscl=1

3. $y = \frac{5}{2} \sin 4x$

Amplitude:

Period:

Frequency:

RANGE
Xmin=-6.28
Xmax=6.28
Xscl=1.57
Ymin=-4
Ymax=4
Yscl=1

Problem Solving Using a Graphing Calculator

This demonstration and worksheet can be used for group instruction or by individual students with graphing calculators. On their worksheets, students are asked to write a function that outputs the height of a Ferris wheel car as a function of time.

The objective of this demonstration and worksheet is to use a trigonometric function to model the height of an object that moves in circular motion.

EXAMPLE FINDING THE HEIGHT OF A FERRIS WHEEL CAR

A Ferris wheel has a diameter of 200 feet and its lowest point is 10 feet above the ground. At full speed, the Ferris wheel rotates once every 30 seconds. Write a model that represents the height, y (in feet), of a car on the Ferris wheel as a function of the time, t (in seconds).

SOLUTION

Let the point $(0, 110)$ represent the center of the Ferris wheel. Let (x, y) represent the location of a car on the Ferris wheel. Then the equation of the circle that represent the wheel is

$$x^2 + (y - 110)^2 = 100^2.$$

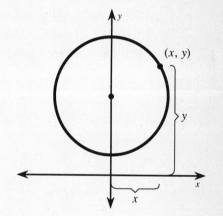

Because the Ferris wheel rotates once every 30 seconds, you know the following relationships between x and t. When $t = 0$, $x = 0$. When $t = 7.5$, $x = 100$. When $t = 15$, $x = 0$. When $t = 22.5$, $x = -100$. When $t = 30$, $x = 0$. A function that models the relationship between x and t is

$$x = 100 \sin(\tfrac{2\pi}{30}t) = 100 \sin(\tfrac{\pi}{15}t).$$

By substituting this expression into the equation of the circle, you obtain the following.

$$(100 \sin(\tfrac{\pi}{15}t))^2 + (y - 110)^2 = 100^2$$

$$(y - 110)^2 = 100^2 - (100 \sin(\tfrac{\pi}{15}t))^2$$

$$(y - 110)^2 = 100^2(1 - \sin^2(\tfrac{\pi}{15}t))$$

$$(y - 110)^2 = 100^2 \cos^2(\tfrac{\pi}{15}t)$$

$$y - 110 = 100 \cos(\tfrac{\pi}{15}t)$$

$$y = 110 + 100 \cos(\tfrac{\pi}{15}t)$$

The graph of this equation is shown below.

RANGE
Xmin=0
Xmax=135
Xscl=10
Ymin=0
Ymax=210
Yscl=10

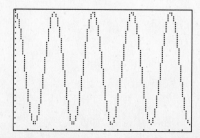

Problem Solving Using a Graphing Calculator

On this worksheet, you are asked to create a model for the height of a car on a Ferris wheel.

EXERCISES

In Exercises 1–7, use the following information.

A Ferris wheel has a diameter of 100 feet and its lowest point is 10 feet above the ground. At full speed, the Ferris wheel rotates once every 40 seconds. Write a model that represents the height, y (in feet), of a car on the Ferris wheel as a function of the time, t (in seconds).

1. Let $(0, \ 60)$ represent the center of the Ferris wheel, and let $(x, \ y)$ represent the location of a car on the Ferris wheel. Write the equation of the circle that represents the Ferris wheel.

2. The variables x and t are related by the equation $x = a \sin bt$. When $t = 0$, $x = 0$. When $t = 10$, $x = 50$. Solve for a and b.

3. Substitute the expression for x that you obtained in Exercise 2 into the equation for the circle that you obtained in Exercise 1. Simplify the result.

4. Solve the equation you obtained in Exercise 3 for y. You should obtain an equation of the form $y = C + A \cos Bt$.

5. Use a graphing calculator to graph the equation you obtained in Exercise 4. Copy the result in the blank screen below.

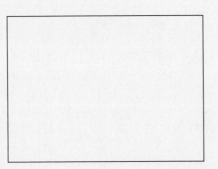

RANGE
Xmin=0
Xmax=120
Xscl=10
Ymin=0
Ymax=120
Yscl=10

6. For the graph in Exercise 5, what does the horizontal axis measure? What does the vertical axis measure?

7. Use the model developed in Exercise 4 to find the height of the Ferris wheel car when $t = 10$, $t = 20$, $t = 30$, and $t = 40$.

Sketching Conics with Parametric Equations	# 14.3

Teacher Demonstration Material

Problem Solving Using a Graphing Calculator

This demonstration and worksheet can be used for group instruction or by individual students with graphing calculators. On their worksheets, students are asked to use a graphing calculator to sketch conics in parametric form.

The objective of this demonstration and worksheet is for students to become familiar with the parametric mode of a graphing calculator.

EXAMPLE   SKETCHING CONICS IN PARAMETRIC MODE

Sketch the graphs of the parametric equations. Identify the resulting conic.

a. $x = 5\cos t,\ y = 2\sin t$ **b.** $x = 5\cos t,\ y = 5\sin t$ **c.** $x = 2\cos t,\ y = 5\sin t$

SOLUTION

To begin, set the graphing calculator to parametric mode and radian mode. Next, enter the following range settings.

Tmin = 0	Xmin=-9	Ymin=-6
Tmax = 6.28	Xmax=9	Ymax=6
Tstep = .1	Xscl=1	Yscl=1

a. Enter the parametric equations $x = 5\cos t$ and $y = 2\sin t$, and activate the graphing feature. You should obtain the following graph.

b. Enter the parametric equations $x = 5\cos t$ and $y = 5\sin t$, and activate the graphing feature. You should obtain the following graph.

c. Enter the parametric equations $x = 2\cos t$ and $y = 5\sin t$, and activate the graphing feature. You should obtain the following graph.

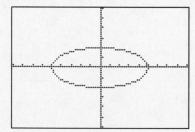   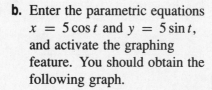 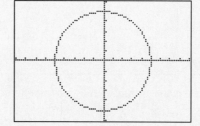   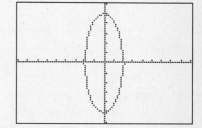

From the display, you can see that this is the graph of an ellipse. To confirm this, write the following.

$$\sin^2 t + \cos^2 t = 1$$
$$\left(\frac{y}{2}\right)^2 + \left(\frac{x}{5}\right)^2 = 1$$
$$\frac{y^2}{2^2} + \frac{x^2}{5^2} = 1$$

From the display, you can see that this is the graph of a circle. To confirm this, write the following.

$$\sin^2 t + \cos^2 t = 1$$
$$\left(\frac{y}{5}\right)^2 + \left(\frac{x}{5}\right)^2 = 1$$
$$y^2 + x^2 = 5^2$$

From the display, you can see that this is the graph of an ellipse. To confirm this, write the following.

$$\sin^2 t + \cos^2 t = 1$$
$$\left(\frac{y}{5}\right)^2 + \left(\frac{x}{2}\right)^2 = 1$$
$$\frac{y^2}{5^2} + \frac{x^2}{2^2} = 1$$

14.3

Name _____

Problem Solving Using a Graphing Calculator

On this worksheet, you are asked to use a graphing calculator to sketch conics in parametric form.

To begin, set the graphing calculator to parametric mode and radian mode. Next, enter the following range settings.

Tmin = 0	Xmin=-9	Ymin=-6
Tmax = 6.28	Xmax=9	Ymax=6
Tstep = .1	Xscl=1	Yscl=1

Finally, enter the parametric equations and activate the graphing feature of the calculator.

EXERCISES

1. Use a graphing calculator to sketch the graph of the parametric equations. Classify the conic as a circle, an ellipse, or a hyperbola. Find the coordinates of the center of the conic.

$x = 4\cos t, y = 6\sin t$

Center: _____

Conic: _____

$x = 6\cos t, y = 6\sin t$

Center: _____

Conic: _____

$x = 6\cos t, y = 4\sin t$

Center: _____

Conic: _____

2. Use a graphing calculator to sketch the graph of the parametric equations. Classify the conic as a circle, an ellipse, or a hyperbola. Find the coordinates of the center of the conic.

$x = 2 + 4\cos t, y = 3 + 3\sin t$

Center: _____

Conic: _____

$x = 2 + 3\cos t, y = -1 + 4\sin t$

Center: _____

Conic: _____

$x = 2\sec t, y = 4\tan t$

Center: _____

Conic: _____

Problem Solving Using a Graphing Calculator

This demonstration and worksheet can be used for group instruction or by individual students with graphing calculators. On their worksheets, students are asked to use a graphing calculator to compute combinations and permutations.

The objective of this demonstration and worksheet is to reinforce the formulas for combinations and permutations by computing them by hand and with a graphing calculator.

EXAMPLE   SELECTING COMMITTEE MEMBERS

You are selecting two people to comprise a committee. You have narrowed the selection down to John, Myles, Glenn, and Von.

a. In how many ways can you select two people from the group of four people?

b. In how many ways can you select two people from the group of four people to be the chair and vice-chair of the committee?

SOLUTION

a. This question can be answered by computing the number of *combinations* of two people taken from a group of four people.

$$_4C_2 = \binom{4}{2} = \frac{4!}{2!2!} = \frac{4 \cdot 3 \cdot 2 \cdot 1}{2 \cdot 1 \cdot 2 \cdot 1} = 6$$

You can verify this in two ways. One way is to actually list all six combinations.

John & Myles	John & Glenn	John & Von
Myles & Glenn	Myles & Von	Glenn & Von

Another way to confirm the result is to use a graphing calculator.

TI-81: 4 $\boxed{\text{MATH}}$ $\boxed{\triangleleft}$ $\boxed{3}$ 2 $\boxed{\text{ENTER}}$ *Display:* 6

CASIO fx-7700G: 4 $\boxed{\text{SHIFT}}$ $\boxed{\text{MATH}}$ $\boxed{\text{F2}}$ $\boxed{\text{F3}}$ 2 $\boxed{\text{EXE}}$ *Display:* 6

b. This question can be answered by computing the number of *permutations* of two people taken from a group of four people.

$$_4P_2 = \frac{4!}{2!} = \frac{4 \cdot 3 \cdot 2 \cdot 1}{2 \cdot 1} = 12$$

You can verify this in two ways. One way is to actually list all twelve combinations.

John & Myles	John & Glenn	John & Von
Myles & John	Glenn & John	Von & John
Myles & Glenn	Myles & Von	Glenn & Von
Glenn & Myles	Von & Myles	Von & Glenn

Another way to confirm the result is to use a graphing calculator.

TI-81: 4 $\boxed{\text{MATH}}$ $\boxed{\triangleleft}$ $\boxed{2}$ 2 $\boxed{\text{ENTER}}$ *Display:* 12

CASIO fx-7700G: 4 $\boxed{\text{SHIFT}}$ $\boxed{\text{MATH}}$ $\boxed{\text{F2}}$ $\boxed{\text{F2}}$ 2 $\boxed{\text{EXE}}$ *Display:* 12

Problem Solving Using a Graphing Calculator

On this worksheet, you are asked to use a graphing calculator to compute combinations and permutations. On the graphing calculator, the number of combinations of n elements taken r at a time is denoted by $_nC_r$ and the number of permutations of n elements taken r at a time is denoted by $_nP_r$. For instance, to compute $_5C_2$, press the following keystrokes (the display should be 10).

TI-81: 5 MATH ◁ 3 2 ENTER

CASIO fx-7700G: 5 SHIFT MATH F2 F3 2 EXE

To compute $_5P_2$, press the following keystrokes (the display should be 20).

TI-81: 5 MATH ◁ 2 2 ENTER

CASIO fx-7700G: 5 SHIFT MATH F2 F2 2 EXE

EXERCISES

In Exercises 1–3, use the following information.

Coston's Pizza Shop offers seven pizza toppings: mushrooms, olives, peppers, onions, sausage, pepperoni, and cheese.

1. Use a graphing calculator to compute the number of combinations of three toppings you can choose from the seven possible toppings.

2. Use a graphing calculator to compute the number of permutations of three toppings you can choose from the seven possible toppings.

3. Would you say that the answer to Exercise 1 or the answer to Exercise 2 would best describe the number of different types of 3-topping pizzas that are available at *Coston's Pizza*? Explain

In Exercises 4–7, complete the table.

	n	r	$n!$	$(n-r)!$	$_nC_r$	$_nP_r$
4.	5	0				
5.	5	5				
6.	5	1				
7.	5	3				

Problem Solving Using a Computer

Program **COINTOSS** is an activity that can be used for group instruction or by individual students with computers that have the BASIC language. In either setting, students should use the accompanying worksheet.

The objective of the program is to show students that the word "random" does *not* mean evenly distributed. For instance, it is possible to flip ten coins and have each coin land "heads up."

The BASIC program listed below simulates the tossing of twelve coins. The experiment is performed 4096 times. Students should understand that the most likely event is that six of the coins will land heads up and six will land tails up. Even with random tosses, however, other outcomes will occur.

BASIC PROGRAM

```
  5   RANDOMIZE
 10   DIM TALLY(13)
 20   FOR N=0 TO 12
 30   TALLY(N)=0
 40   NEXT
 50   FOR I=1 TO 4096
 60   HEADS=0
 70   FOR J=1 TO 12
 80   COIN=RND(J)
 90   IF COIN<.5 THEN HEADS=HEADS+1
100   NEXT
110   TALLY(HEADS)=TALLY(HEADS)+1
115   IF I/50 = INT(I/50) THEN PRINT "GAMES COMPLETED "; I
120   NEXT
130   FOR N=0 TO 12
140   PRINT "NUMBER OF GAMES WITH  ";N;" HEADS  ";TALLY(N)
150   NEXT
160   END
```

When this program is run, the user will be prompted to enter a number that "seeds" the computer's random number generator. After that, the computer will perform 4096 experiments and finally print the results. One possible outcome is shown at the right. Check your computer manual to determine how your specific computer generates random numbers. Adjust lines 5 and 80 accordingly.

NUMBER OF GAMES WITH		HEADS	
NUMBER OF GAMES WITH	0	HEADS	1
NUMBER OF GAMES WITH	1	HEADS	12
NUMBER OF GAMES WITH	2	HEADS	77
NUMBER OF GAMES WITH	3	HEADS	238
NUMBER OF GAMES WITH	4	HEADS	502
NUMBER OF GAMES WITH	5	HEADS	759
NUMBER OF GAMES WITH	6	HEADS	961
NUMBER OF GAMES WITH	7	HEADS	761
NUMBER OF GAMES WITH	8	HEADS	491
NUMBER OF GAMES WITH	9	HEADS	208
NUMBER OF GAMES WITH	10	HEADS	65
NUMBER OF GAMES WITH	11	HEADS	20
NUMBER OF GAMES WITH	12	HEADS	1

15.4

Name _____

*Problem Solving
Using a Computer*

A computer program can be used to simulate probability experiments. On this worksheet, you are asked to use a computer program that simulates the tossing of 12 coins. This particular program tosses twelve coins 4096 times and then prints a frequency distribution for the number of heads that occurred on each toss.

EXERCISES

1. Run the program COINTOSS. Record your results below.

   NUMBER OF GAMES WITH 0 HEADS _____
   NUMBER OF GAMES WITH 1 HEADS _____
   NUMBER OF GAMES WITH 2 HEADS _____
   NUMBER OF GAMES WITH 3 HEADS _____
   NUMBER OF GAMES WITH 4 HEADS _____
   NUMBER OF GAMES WITH 5 HEADS _____
   NUMBER OF GAMES WITH 6 HEADS _____
   NUMBER OF GAMES WITH 7 HEADS _____
   NUMBER OF GAMES WITH 8 HEADS _____
   NUMBER OF GAMES WITH 9 HEADS _____
   NUMBER OF GAMES WITH 10 HEADS _____
   NUMBER OF GAMES WITH 11 HEADS _____
   NUMBER OF GAMES WITH 12 HEADS _____

2. According to the *experimental* results obtained in Exercise 1, what is the probability that when 12 coins are tossed, exactly 2 will land heads up?

3. The *theoretical* numbers of ways that 12 coins can land heads up (when tossed 4096 times) is given by the 12th row of Pascal's Triangle. Complete the following.

   NUMBER OF GAMES WITH 0 HEADS $\binom{12}{0} =$ _____
   NUMBER OF GAMES WITH 1 HEADS $\binom{12}{1} =$ _____
   NUMBER OF GAMES WITH 2 HEADS $\binom{12}{2} =$ _____
   NUMBER OF GAMES WITH 3 HEADS $\binom{12}{3} =$ _____
   NUMBER OF GAMES WITH 4 HEADS $\binom{12}{4} =$ _____
   NUMBER OF GAMES WITH 5 HEADS $\binom{12}{5} =$ _____
   NUMBER OF GAMES WITH 6 HEADS $\binom{12}{6} =$ _____
   NUMBER OF GAMES WITH 7 HEADS $\binom{12}{7} =$ _____
   NUMBER OF GAMES WITH 8 HEADS $\binom{12}{8} =$ _____
   NUMBER OF GAMES WITH 9 HEADS $\binom{12}{9} =$ _____
   NUMBER OF GAMES WITH 10 HEADS $\binom{12}{10} =$ _____
   NUMBER OF GAMES WITH 11 HEADS $\binom{12}{11} =$ _____
   NUMBER OF GAMES WITH 12 HEADS $\binom{12}{12} =$ _____

4. According to the *theoretical* results obtained in Exercise 3, what is the probability that when 12 coins are tossed, exactly 2 will land heads up?

APPENDIX A: TI-81 KEYSTROKES

Symbol	Keystrokes
+	[+]
−	[−]
*	[×]
/	[÷]
-	[(-)]
^{2}	[x^2]
^{3}	[MATH] [3]
^	[^]
(	[(]
)	[)]
Space	[ALPHA] [␣]
,	[ALPHA] [,]
"	[ALPHA] ["]
?	[ALPHA] [?]
!	[MATH] [5]
→	[STO▷]
X	[X|T] or [ALPHA] [X]
=	[2nd] [TEST] [1]
≠	[2nd] [TEST] [2]
>	[2nd] [TEST] [3]
≥	[2nd] [TEST] [4]
<	[2nd] [TEST] [5]
≤	[2nd] [TEST] [6]
Y_1	[2nd] [Y-VARS] [1]
Y_2	[2nd] [Y-VARS] [2]
Y_3	[2nd] [Y-VARS] [3]
Y_4	[2nd] [Y-VARS] [4]

Function	Keystrokes
π	[2nd] [π]
abs	[2nd] [ABS]
√	[2nd] [√]
[A]	[2nd] [A]
[B]	[2nd] [B]
[C]	[2nd] [C]
1-Var	[2nd] [STAT] [1] [ENTER]
LinReg	[2nd] [STAT] [2] [ENTER]
LnReg	[2nd] [STAT] [3] [ENTER]
ExpReg	[2nd] [STAT] [4] [ENTER]
PwrReg	[2nd] [STAT] [5] [ENTER]
Hist	[2nd] [STAT] [▷] [1] [ENTER]
Scatter	[2nd] [STAT] [▷] [2] [ENTER]
ClrStat	[2nd] [STAT] [◁] [2] [ENTER]
ClrDraw	[2nd] [DRAW] [1] [ENTER]
Fix	[MODE] [4]
Float	[MODE] [5]
Rad	[MODE] [6]
All-On	[2nd] [Y-VARS] [▷] [1]
All-Off	[2nd] [Y-VARS] [◁] [1]
Pt-On(	[2nd] [DRAW] [3]
DrawF	[2nd] [DRAW] [6]
Param	[MODE] [▷] [2]
Function	[MODE] [▷] [1]
Grid Off	[MODE] [▷] [7]

Function	Keystrokes
Xmin	[VARS] [◁] [1]
Xmax	[VARS] [◁] [2]
Xscl	[VARS] [◁] [3]
Ymin	[VARS] [◁] [4]
Ymax	[VARS] [◁] [5]
Yscl	[VARS] [◁] [6]
Round(	[MATH] [▷] [1]
IPart	[MATH] [▷] [2]
FPart	[MATH] [▷] [3]
Int	[MATH] [▷] [4]
Rand	[MATH] [◁] [1]
RowSwap(	[MATRX] [1]
Row+(	[MATRX] [2]
*Row(	[MATRX] [3]
*Row+(	[MATRX] [4]
Lbl	[PRGM] [1]
Goto	[PRGM] [2]
If	[PRGM] [3]
Pause	[PRGM] [6]
End	[PRGM] [7]
Stop	[PRGM] [8]
Disp	[PRGM] [▷] [1]
Input	[PRGM] [▷] [2]
DispGraph	[PRGM] [▷] [4]
ClrHome	[PRGM] [▷] [5]

NOTES

1. Commands that begin with [PRGM] can be accessed only while editing a program.

2. Letters of the alphabet can be accessed by pressing [ALPHA] and the letter (except when using the store key, then press only the letter).

3. To enter data in statistical memory, press [2nd] [STAT] [◁] [ENTER]. Ordered pairs are entered $x1$, $y1$, $x2$, $y2$, and so on. If data is one-dimensional, enter 1 for each yi.

3. To set zoom factors, press [ZOOM] [4], enter x-factor, press [ENTER], enter y-factor, press [ENTER] [2nd] [QUIT].

MODES

The standard modes are shown boxed at the right. To change a mode, press [MODE], cursor to the desired mode, and press [ENTER].

[Norm]	Sci	Eng
[Float]	0123456789	
[Rad]	Deg	
[Function]	Param	
[Connected]	Dot	
[Sequence]	Simul	
[Grid Off]	Grid On	
[Rect]	Polar	

+	$\boxed{+}$	2	$\boxed{\text{SHIFT}}\ \boxed{x^2}$	≤	$\boxed{\text{SHIFT}}\ \boxed{\text{PRGM}}\ \boxed{\text{F2}}\ \boxed{\text{F6}}$
−	$\boxed{-}$	,	$\boxed{\text{SHIFT}}\ \boxed{,}$	π	$\boxed{\text{SHIFT}}\ \boxed{\pi}$
×	$\boxed{\times}$	!	$\boxed{\text{SHIFT}}\ \boxed{\text{MATH}}\ \boxed{\text{F2}}\ \boxed{\text{F1}}$	⇒	$\boxed{\text{SHIFT}}\ \boxed{\text{PRGM}}\ \boxed{\text{F1}}\ \boxed{\text{F1}}$
÷	$\boxed{\div}$	?	$\boxed{\text{SHIFT}}\ \boxed{\text{PRGM}}\ \boxed{\text{F4}}$	Abs	$\boxed{\text{SHIFT}}\ \boxed{\text{MATH}}\ \boxed{\text{F3}}\ \boxed{\text{F1}}$
→	$\boxed{\rightarrow}$	:	$\boxed{\text{SHIFT}}\ \boxed{\text{PRGM}}\ \boxed{\text{F6}}$	Int	$\boxed{\text{SHIFT}}\ \boxed{\text{MATH}}\ \boxed{\text{F3}}\ \boxed{\text{F2}}$
√	$\boxed{\sqrt{\ }}$	◢	$\boxed{\text{SHIFT}}\ \boxed{\text{PRGM}}\ \boxed{5}$	Ran#	$\boxed{\text{SHIFT}}\ \boxed{\text{MATH}}\ \boxed{\text{F2}}\ \boxed{\text{F4}}$
x^y	$\boxed{x^y}$	X	$\boxed{\text{X},\theta,\text{T}}$ or $\boxed{\text{ALPHA}}\ \boxed{\text{X}}$	Lbl	$\boxed{\text{SHIFT}}\ \boxed{\text{PRGM}}\ \boxed{\text{F1}}\ \boxed{\text{F3}}$
(	$\boxed{(}$	=	$\boxed{\text{SHIFT}}\ \boxed{\text{PRGM}}\ \boxed{\text{F2}}\ \boxed{\text{F1}}$	Goto	$\boxed{\text{SHIFT}}\ \boxed{\text{PRGM}}\ \boxed{\text{F1}}\ \boxed{\text{F2}}$
)	$\boxed{)}$	≠	$\boxed{\text{SHIFT}}\ \boxed{\text{PRGM}}\ \boxed{\text{F2}}\ \boxed{\text{F2}}$	Fix	$\boxed{\text{SHIFT}}\ \boxed{\text{DISP}}\ \boxed{\text{F1}}$
Space	$\boxed{\text{ALPHA}}\ \boxed{\text{SPACE}}$	>	$\boxed{\text{SHIFT}}\ \boxed{\text{PRGM}}\ \boxed{\text{F2}}\ \boxed{\text{F3}}$	Norm	$\boxed{\text{SHIFT}}\ \boxed{\text{DISP}}\ \boxed{\text{F3}}$
"	$\boxed{\text{ALPHA}}\ \boxed{\text{F2}}$	<	$\boxed{\text{SHIFT}}\ \boxed{\text{PRGM}}\ \boxed{\text{F2}}\ \boxed{\text{F4}}$	Cls	$\boxed{\text{SHIFT}}\ \boxed{\text{F5}}$
-	$\boxed{\text{SHIFT}}\ \boxed{(-)}$	≥	$\boxed{\text{SHIFT}}\ \boxed{\text{PRGM}}\ \boxed{\text{F2}}\ \boxed{\text{F5}}$	RAD	$\boxed{\text{SHIFT}}\ \boxed{\text{DRG}}\ \boxed{\text{F2}}$

Letters of the alphabet can be accessed by pressing $\boxed{\text{ALPHA}}$ and the letter.

To clear a graphic display:	$\boxed{\text{SHIFT}}\ \boxed{\text{F5}}\ \boxed{\text{EXE}}$
To enter equation-graphing mode:	$\boxed{\text{MODE}}\ \boxed{\text{SHIFT}}\ \boxed{+}$
To enter inequality-graphing mode:	$\boxed{\text{MODE}}\ \boxed{\text{SHIFT}}\ \boxed{\div}$
To edit a program:	$\boxed{\text{MODE}}\ \boxed{2}$, Cursor to program, $\boxed{\text{EXE}}$
To run a program:	$\boxed{\text{SHIFT}}\ \boxed{\text{PRGM}}\ \boxed{\text{F3}}$, Press program number
To enter linear regression mode:	$\boxed{\text{MODE}}\ \boxed{4}$
To enter exponential regression mode:	$\boxed{\text{MODE}}\ \boxed{6}$
To enter power regression mode:	$\boxed{\text{MODE}}\ \boxed{7}$
To enter matrix mode:	$\boxed{\text{MODE}}\ \boxed{0}$
To enter arithmetic calculation mode:	$\boxed{\text{MODE}}\ \boxed{+}$
Normal display format:	$\boxed{\text{SHIFT}}\ \boxed{\text{DISP}}\ \boxed{\text{F3}}\ \boxed{\text{EXE}}$
Change significant digits:	$\boxed{\text{SHIFT}}\ \boxed{\text{DISP}}\ \boxed{\text{F1}}$, Number of digits, $\boxed{\text{EXE}}$
To set zoom factors:	$\boxed{\text{SHIFT}}\ \boxed{\text{F2}}\ \boxed{\text{F2}}$, x factor, $\boxed{\text{EXE}}$, y factor, $\boxed{\text{EXE}}$

To enter 1-variable statistics. (Standard deviation mode) $\boxed{\text{MODE}}\ \boxed{\times}$

To store data:	$\boxed{\text{MODE}}\ \boxed{\text{SHIFT}}\ \boxed{1}$
To use data without storing:	$\boxed{\text{MODE}}\ \boxed{\text{SHIFT}}\ \boxed{2}$
To draw statistical graph:	$\boxed{\text{MODE}}\ \boxed{\text{SHIFT}}\ \boxed{3}$
To clear data in storage:	$\boxed{\text{MODE}}\ \boxed{\text{SHIFT}}\ \boxed{1}\ \boxed{\text{F2}}\ \boxed{\text{F3}}\ \boxed{\text{F1}}$
To clear data not in storage:	$\boxed{\text{SHIFT}}\ \boxed{\text{CLR}}\ \boxed{\text{F2}}\ \boxed{\text{EXE}}$

To enter 2-variable statistics. (Regression mode) $\boxed{\text{MODE}}\ \boxed{\div}$

To store data:	$\boxed{\text{MODE}}\ \boxed{\text{SHIFT}}\ \boxed{1}$
To use data without storing:	$\boxed{\text{MODE}}\ \boxed{\text{SHIFT}}\ \boxed{2}$
To draw statistical graph:	$\boxed{\text{MODE}}\ \boxed{\text{SHIFT}}\ \boxed{3}$
To clear data in storage:	$\boxed{\text{MODE}}\ \boxed{\text{SHIFT}}\ \boxed{1}\ \boxed{\text{F2}}\ \boxed{\text{F3}}\ \boxed{\text{F1}}$
To clear data not in storage:	$\boxed{\text{SHIFT}}\ \boxed{\text{CLR}}\ \boxed{\text{F2}}\ \boxed{\text{EXE}}$

ANSWERS TO WORKSHEETS

■ **Worksheet 1.1**

1.

	TI-81	CASIO fx-7700G
Darker:	2nd △ (hold)	MODE ▷
Lighter:	2nd ▽ (hold)	MODE ◁

2.

TI-81	CASIO fx-7700G
X|T or ALPHA X	X,θ,T or ALPHA X

3.

	TI-81	CASIO fx-7700G
a.	8 STO▷ X|T ENTER	8 → X,θ,T EXE
b.	21 STO▷ A ENTER	21 → ALPHA A EXE
c.	(-) 6 STO▷ E ENTER	SHIFT (-) 6 → ALPHA E EXE
d.	100 STO▷ I ENTER	100 → ALPHA I EXE
e.	2nd π STO▷ O ENTER	SHIFT π → ALPHA O EXE
f.	1.1 x^2 STO▷ U ENTER	1.1 SHIFT x^2 → ALPHA U EXE

4. 1728.771429   **5.** Answers vary.

6. The sum of the products of the values stored in the variables of your first and last names.

7. *TI-81:* △   *CASIO fx-7700G:* ◁

8. The difference of the products of the values stored in the variables of your first and last names.

9. The sum of the values stored in the variables of your first name.

10. a. 32 **b.** 1005.309649 **c.** 148.78 **d.** 5.49 **e.** 5.433628319 **f.** 7.0525

11. 102.2   **12.** 21.11111111

■ **Worksheet 1.8**

1. d   2. 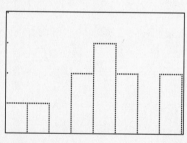   **3.** 4.25   **4.** 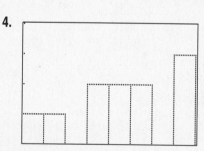   **5.** 4.5

■ **Worksheet 2.2**   (Answers vary.)   ■ **Worksheet 2.6(1)**   (Answers vary.)

■ **Worksheet 2.6(2)**

1. Right 5 units; Up 8 units; Reflection.
None; Down 2 units; None.
Right 5 units; None; None.
Left 2 units; Up 9 units; Reflection.
Left 3 units; Down 4 units; None.
Left 12 units; None; None.

2. (5, 8); (0, -2); (5, 0);
(-2, 9); (-3, -4); (-12, 0)

3.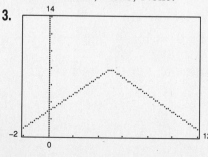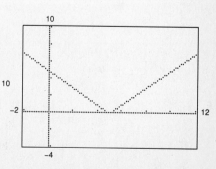

3. (Continued)

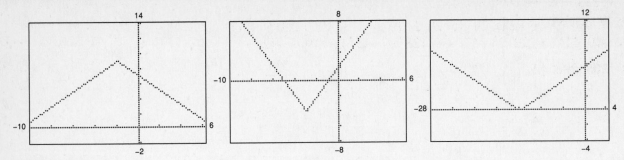

■ Worksheet 2.7

1. Answers vary.

2. Answers vary.

3. 0.1; 0.973; 0.913; $y = 0.1 + 0.973x$

4.

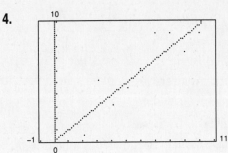

5.
$$x_i - \overline{x}:\quad -4.5,\quad -3.5,\quad -2.5,\quad -1.5,\quad -0.5,$$
$$0.5,\quad 1.5,\quad 2.5,\quad 3.5,\quad 4.5;\quad 0$$
$$(x_i - \overline{x})^2:\quad 20.25,\quad 12.25,\quad 6.25,\quad 2.25,\quad 0.25,$$
$$0.25,\quad 2.25,\quad 6.25,\quad 12.25,\quad 20.25;\quad 82.50$$
$$y_i - \overline{y}:\quad -4.45,\quad -4.95,\quad -0.45,\quad -2,45,\quad -0.95,$$
$$0.55,\quad 3.55,\quad 3.55,\quad 2.05,\quad 3.55;\quad 0$$
$$(y_i - \overline{y})^2:\ 19.8025,\ 24.5025,\ 0.2025,\ 6.0025,\ 0.9025,$$
$$0.3025,\ 12.6025,\ 12.6025,\ 4.2025,\ 12.6025;\quad 93.725$$
$$(x_i - \overline{x})(y_i - \overline{x}):\quad 20.025,\quad 17.325,\quad 1.125,\quad 3.675,\quad 0.475,$$
$$0.275,\quad 5.325,\quad 8.875,\quad 7.175,\quad 15.975;\quad 80.25$$

6. 0.913

■ Worksheet 3.1

1. c   **2.** a   **3.** d   **4.** b   **5.** (4, 2)   **6.** (-1, 3)   **7.** (5, -5)

8. (-1, -3)   **9.** $4800 at 5%, $1200 at 8%

■ Worksheet 4.4(1)

1. a. 1 **b.** 1 **c.** 2   **2.** Same as Exercise 1   **3.** You get an error message. A nonsquare matrix does not have a determinant.

4. a. $\begin{bmatrix} 3 & 4 \\ 5 & 7 \end{bmatrix}$ **b.** $\begin{bmatrix} 1 & -2 \\ -2 & 5 \end{bmatrix}$ **c.** $\begin{bmatrix} -1 & 1 \\ -3.5 & 3 \end{bmatrix}$ **5.** $A \times A^{-1} = \begin{bmatrix} 1 & 0 \\ 0 & 1 \end{bmatrix} = A^{-1} \times A$

6. Same as Exercise 4

■ Worksheet 4.4(2)

1. 23 5 12 12 0 4 15 14 5 0   **2.** -31 -49 12 12 12 16 12 11 -10 -15

3. 360 DATA "WELL DONE"   **4.** WELL DONE; 23 5 12 12 0 4 15 14 5 0;
370 DATA -2,-3,3,4   -31 -49 12 12 12 16 12 11 -10 -15;
These results are the same as those in Exercises 1 and 2.

5. SEND MONEY; 19 5 14 4 0 13 15 14 5 25;
110 -153 82 -114 39 -52 117 -161 100 -135

6. HOME SWEET HOME; 8 15 13 5 0 19 23 5 5 20 0 8 15 13 5 0;
-82 67 -17 12 -114 95 -7 2 -115 95 -48 40 -63 50 5 -5

7. OVER THE HILL; 15 22 5 18 0 20 8 5 0 8 9 12 12 0;
68 83 12 17 -20 -20 43 51 -8 -8 42 51 72 84

8. ROSES ARE RED; 18 15 19 5 19 0 1 18 5 0 18 5 4 0;
-39 51 13 -22 38 -57 -88 123 10 -15 11 -19 8 -12

■ **Worksheet 4.6**

1. (3, -2)   **2.** (1, 2)   **3.** (-4, -1)   **4.** (3, -6)

5. (6, 1, -3)   **6.** (-1, 5, 2)   **7.** (2, 0, -9)

■ **Worksheet 5.2(1)**   (Answers vary.)

■ **Worksheet 5.2(2)**

1.
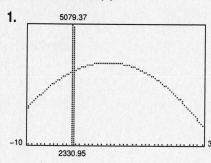

2.
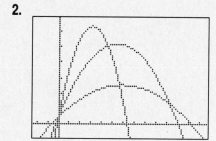

3. 35°

4. 75°

5. 75°

6.
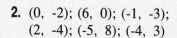

■ **Worksheet 5.3**

1. None; Down 2 units; None.
Right 6 units; None; None.
Left 1 unit; Down 3 units; None.
Right 2 units; Down 4 units; Reflection.
Left 5 units; Up 8 units; Reflection.
Left 4 units; Up 3 units; None.

2. (0, -2); (6, 0); (-1, -3);
(2, -4); (-5, 8); (-4, 3)

3.
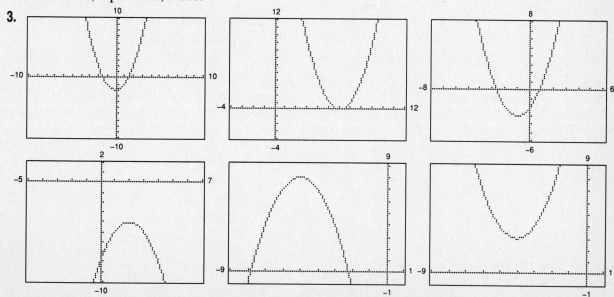

■ **Worksheet 5.4**

1. $H = -16t^2 + 90t + 15$ 2. $a = -16, b = 90, c = 15$ 3. -0.162   4. 5.787

5. No, the negative value for time does not make sense.   6. d

7. **a.** The discriminant must be enclosed in parentheses; -0.2922512109

   b. The numerator must be enclosed in parentheses; -1.951941016

   c. -45 must be enclosed in parentheses; -5.276332565

8. The second 1; the division symbol "/"

■ **Worksheet 6.2**

1. $y = 3x^3 + 4.4x^2 - 14x + 6.1$ 4.   5. -96.78, 3.44

2. **b**

3. -3.15, 0.59, 1.10

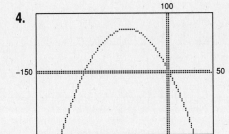

■ **Worksheet 6.5**

1. $y = |x| - 6$ 2. $y = -(x + 1)^2$ 3. $y = \sqrt{x + 3}$ 4. $y = x^3 + 2$

5. The graph of $y = x^2$ is reflected in the x-axis and shifted 3 units down.

6. The graph of $y = |x|$ is shifted 4 units to the left.

7. The graph of $y = \sqrt{x}$ is shifted 2 units down.

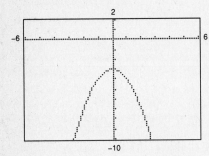

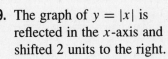

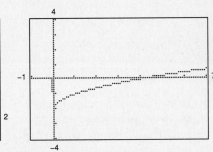

8. The graph of $y = x^2$ is shifted 1 unit to the right and 1 unit up.

9. The graph of $y = |x|$ is reflected in the x-axis and shifted 2 units to the right.

10. The graph of $y = x^3$ is shifted 1 unit to the left.

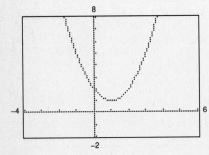

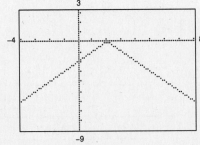

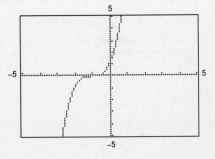

11. The graph of $y = \sqrt{x}$ is reflected in the x-axis and shifted 1 unit to the left.

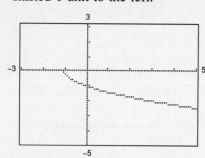

12. The graph of $y = x^2$ is reflected in the x-axis, shifted 2 units to the left, and 3 units up.

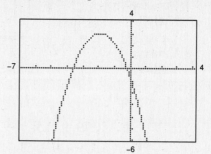

■ **Worksheet 6.7**

1.

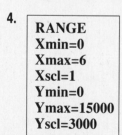

2. 4; the mode is equal to 4.

3. 3.55

4. 4

5. Median or mode

6. 4.2;

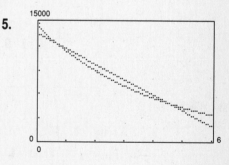

■ **Worksheet 7.2(1)**   (Answers vary.)

■ **Worksheet 7.2(2)**

1. (0, 14280), (1, 11200), (2, 8900), (5, 4300)

2. Linear: $a = 13507.1$, $b = -1918.6$, $r = -0.986$, $y = 13507.1 - 1918.6x$

Exponential: $a = 14289.8$, $b = 0.787$, $r = -1.000$, $y = 14289.8(0.787)^x$

3. Exponential, because $|r|$ is closer to 1 for the exponential model.

4.

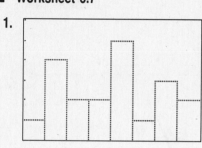

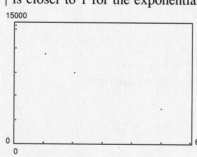

5.

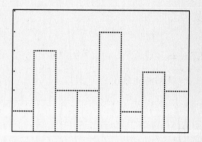

6. 2.9 years   **7.** $y = 14289.8\left(\frac{1}{2}\right)^{x/2.9}$

8. a. 2.9 years   **b.** 5.8 years   **c.** 11.1 years   **d.** 14.0 years

■ **Worksheet 7.5**

1. a. $y = \sqrt{5x} - 11$ **b.**

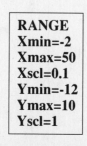

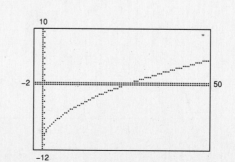

c. 24.2

2. a. $y = \sqrt{\frac{3}{2}x + 1} - 3$ **b.**

RANGE
Xmin=-4
Xmax=8
Xscl=0.1
Ymin=-4
Ymax=8
Yscl=1

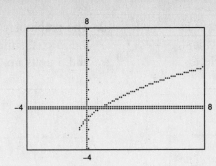

c. 0.8

■ **Worksheet 8.5**

1. a.

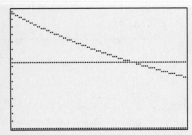

b. 5.279; 9.255; 0.992; $5.279 + 9.255 \ln x$

c.

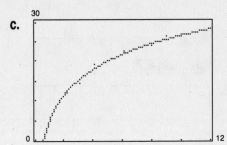

2. $y = -628.56 + 4069.96 \ln x$ **3.** 10,656 million dollars

■ **Worksheet 8.6**

1. a.

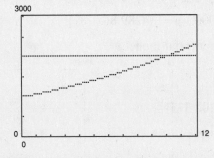

b. 14,110   **c.** 14,109.7

2. 9.9 years; Yes

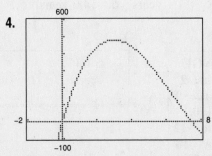

■ **Worksheet 9.2**

1. a   **2. a.** True **b.** False **c.** True
d. False **e.** True **f.** True
g. False **h.** False **i.** False

3. $y = (15 - 2x)(24 - 2x)(x)$ **4.**

5. 486 in^3; 3 in. × 3 in.
6. 3.5 cm; 421.9 cm^3

■ Worksheet 9.3

1. $y = (x + 2)(x + 1)(x - 3)$
$y = x^3 - 7x - 6$

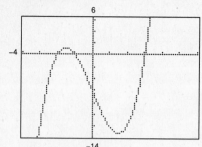

2. $y = (x - 4)(x - 1)(x + 1)$

3. $y = (x)(x + 1)(x - 3)$

4. $y = (x - 5)(x - 2)(x + 1)(x + 3)$

5. a, b, c, and d

6. No

7. Graph touches x-axis at $x = 2$.   Graph crosses x-axis at $x = 2$.   Graph touches x-axis at $x = 2$.

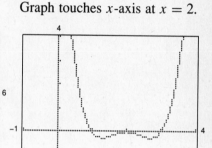

■ Worksheet 9.4

1. Row 2: A1∗B3, A1∗C3, A1∗D3, A1∗E3
Row 3: B1, C1+C2, D1+D2, E1+E2, F1+F2

2. $2x^3 - 3x^2 + x - 4$

3.
$$
\begin{array}{r}
2x^3 - 3x^2 + x - 4 \\
x - 2 \overline{)2x^4 - 7x^3 + 7x^2 - 6x + 8} \\
\underline{2x^4 - 4x^3} \\
-3x^3 + 7x^2 \\
\underline{-3x^3 + 6x^2} \\
x^2 - 6x \\
\underline{x^2 - 2x} \\
-4x + 8 \\
\underline{-4x + 8} \\
0
\end{array}
$$

4. $x^3 + 2x^2 - x + 1$

5. $3x^3 - 2x^2 + 1$

6. $x^2 + 9x - 5$

7. $-2x^2 + 7x - 1$

8. $-1, -\frac{3}{2}, 2$

9. $-1, -2, \frac{7}{3}$

10. 375

11. 25

■ Worksheet 9.5

1. $-\frac{9}{2}$, -4, -2, $-\frac{3}{2}$, 3   **2.** -5, $-\frac{10}{3}$, -3, -1, $\frac{8}{3}$, 3   **3.** $-\frac{3}{2}$, $-\frac{4}{3}$, $\frac{1}{2}$, $\frac{1}{3}$, 3

4.
$-\frac{9}{2}$, 0, 3, -22.5;			No
-4, 2, 3, 0;	$2x^2 - 3x - 9$;	Yes
-2, 1, 2, 5;		No
$-\frac{3}{2}$, 2, 2, 0;	$2x - 6$;	Yes
3, 1, 1, 0;	2;	Yes

$y = (x + 4)(x + \frac{3}{2})(x - 3)$

5.
-5, 0, 4, 0;	$3x^3 + 4x^2 - 23x - 24$;	Yes
$-\frac{10}{3}$, 1, 3, -14;		No
-3, 2, 3, 0;	$3x^2 - 5x - 8$;	Yes
-1, 1, 2, 0;	$3x - 8$;	Yes
$\frac{8}{3}$, 1, 1, 0;	3;	Yes
3, 1, 4, 3;		No

$y = (x + 5)(x + 3)(x + 1)(x - \frac{8}{3})$

6. $-\frac{3}{2}$, 0, 3, -9;   No   **7.** $\frac{1}{3}$, $\frac{1}{2}$, 1, 12, $\sqrt{5}$, $-\sqrt{5}$

     $-\frac{4}{3}$, 2, 3, 0; $6x^2 - 21x + 9$;   Yes

     $\frac{1}{2}$, 1, 2, 0; $6x - 18$;   Yes

     $\frac{1}{3}$, 1, 1, -16;   No

     3, 2, 1, 0;   6;   Yes

     $y = (x + \frac{4}{3})(x - \frac{1}{2})(x - 3)$

■ Worksheet 9.6

Games 1–3 (Answers vary.)

1. c; 0, 2, -4   **2.** $y = x^3 + 2x^2 - 8x$

■ Worksheet 9.7

1. 4   **2.** 2   **3.** $x_i - \overline{x}$: 2, -1, -2, -1, 0, 1, 0, 2, -2, 1; 0   **4.** 1.414

                         $(x_i - \overline{x})^2$: 4, 1, 4, 1, 0, 1, 0, 4, 4, 1; 20

                   1.414

5.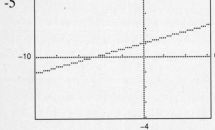

6. 3.5; 1.893

7. a. (1.607, 5.393)

    b. (-0.286, 7.286)

    c. (-2.179, 9.179)

8. $(\overline{x} - s, \overline{x} + s)$:   12, 66.7%

    $(\overline{x} - 2s, \overline{x} + 2s)$:   18, 100%

    $(\overline{x} - 3s, \overline{x} + 3s)$:   18, 100%

■ Worksheet 10.4

1. -5

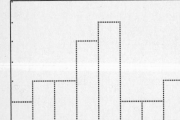

2. 5

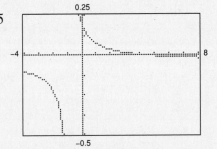

3. 4

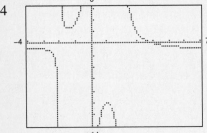

4. 1, 3

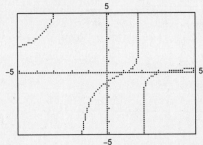

5. -2, 2   **6.** -2   **7.** 0, -2   **8.** -2, 5

■ Worksheet 10.6(1)

1. $64.31   **2.** 40   RAT=.08

                     50   BAL=560

                     60   PAY=64.31

3.

$560.00	$64.31	$3.73	$60.58	$499.42
$499.42	$64.31	$3.33	$60.98	$438.44
$438.44	$64.31	$2.92	$61.39	$377.05
$377.05	$64.31	$2.51	$61.80	$315.25
$315.25	$64.31	$2.10	$62.21	$253.04
$253.04	$64.31	$1.69	$62.62	$190.42
$190.42	$64.31	$1.27	$63.04	$127.38
$127.38	$64.31	$0.85	$63.46	$63.92
$63.92	$64.35	$0.43	$63.92	$0.00

4. 60 MON=6
70 PAY=95.52

5.

$560.00	$95.52	$3.73	$91.79	$468.21
$468.21	$95.52	$3.12	$92.40	$375.81
$375.81	$95.52	$2.51	$93.01	$282.80
$282.80	$95.52	$1.89	$93.63	$189.17
$189.80	$95.52	$1.26	$94.26	$94.91
$94.91	$95.54	$0.63	$94.91	$0.00

$5.69

■ **Worksheet 10.6(2)**

1. $44,500; $548.47; $54,224.60; Yes

2. $108,260; $1,229.99; $186,937.60; No

3. $123,500; $1,048.43; $128,123.20; Yes

4. $123,500; $1,127.10; $147,004.00; No

■ **Worksheet 11.2**

1. $y = \sqrt{25 - x^2}$ is the upper half.
$y = -\sqrt{25 - x^2}$ is the bottom half.

2. y is not a function of x. To be a function, there must be only one value of y for each value of x.

3. 5; (-5, 0) and (5, 0); (0, -5) and (0, 5)

4.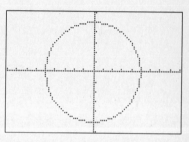

The second range appears circular because it is a square setting. A square setting means that there are equal spaces between tic marks.

5.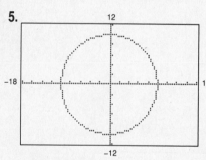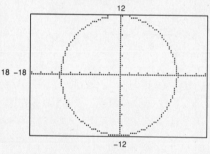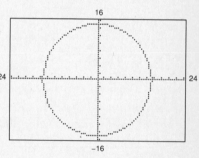

6. (24, 10), (10, 24)   **7.** (8, 6), (6, 8)   **8.** (0, -4)

■ **Worksheet 11.3**

1. a. 0.52   **b.** 0.75   **c.** 0.97

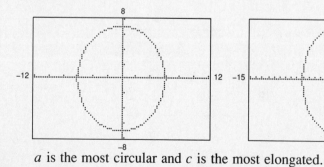 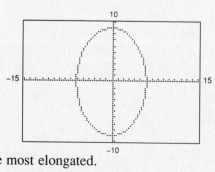 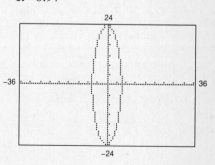

a is the most circular and c is the most elongated.

2.

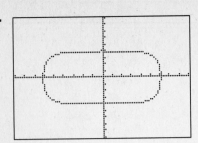

3. No; Yes

■ **Worksheet 11.5**

1. Circle, (2, 2)

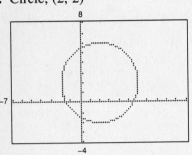

Hyperbola, (2, 2)

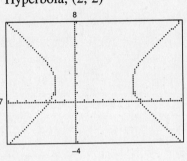

Ellipse, (2, 2)

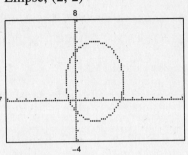

2. Hyperbola, (3, -2)

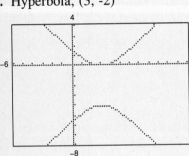

Ellipse, (3, -2)

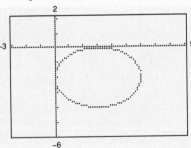

Ellipse, (3, -2)

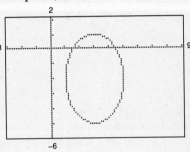

■ **Worksheet 12.4(1)**

1. 1st 5 terms: 120, 144, 172.8, 207.36, 248.832
Partial sums: 120, 264, 436.8, 644.16, 892.992
Series has no sum; Yscl = 4000

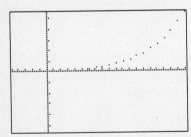

2. 1st 5 terms: 65, 65, 65, 65, 65
Partial sums: 65, 130, 195, 260, 325
Series has no sum; Yscl = 100

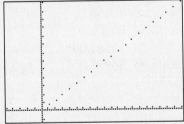

3. 1st 5 terms: 5000, 4000, 3200, 2560, 2048
Partial sums: 5000, 9000, 12,200, 14,760, 16,808
Series sum is 25,000; Yscl = 3000

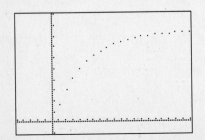

4. 1st 5 terms: 50, 25, 12.5, 6.25, 3.125
Partial sums: 50, 75, 87.5, 93.75, 96.875
Series sum is 100; Yscl = 20

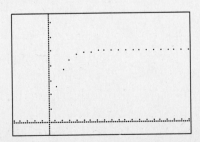

116 *Answers to Worksheets* ■

5. 1st 5 terms: 100, 0, 0, 0, 0
Partial sums: 100, 100, 100, 100, 100
Series sum is 100; Yscl = 20

6. 1st 5 terms: 8, -4.8, 2.88, -1.728, 1.0368
Partial sums: 8, 3.2, 6.08, 4.352, 5.3888
Series sum is 5; Yscl = 0.5

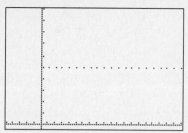

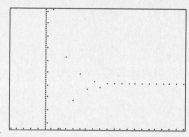

7. 1st 5 terms: 100, -95, 90.25, -85.74, 81.45
Partial sums: 100, 5, 95.25, 9.51, 90.96
Series sum is 51.3; Yscl = 10

8. 1st 5 terms: 400, -400, 400, -400, 400
Partial sums: 400, 0, 400, 0, 400
Series has no sum; Yscl = 50

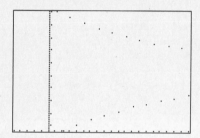

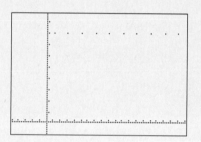

■ **Worksheet 12.4(2)**

In 1–7, (Answers vary.)   **8.** If $|r| \geq 1$, then the series has no sum. Otherwise, the series has a sum. No; Yes.

■ **Worksheet 12.5**

1. 1, 9, 36, 84, 126, 126, 84, 36, 9, 1   **2.** $x^7y^2, x^6y^3, x^5y^4, x^4y^5, x^3y^6, x^2y^7, x^1y^8, x^0y^9$

3. $x^9 + 9x^8y + 36x^7y^2 + 84x^6y^3 + 126x^5y^4 + 126x^4y^5 + 84x^3y^6 + 36x^2y^7 + 9xy^8 + y^9$

4. 1, 7, 21, 35, 35, 21, 7, 1   **5.** $(2x)^5(1)^2, (2x)^4(1)^3, (2x)^3(1)^4, (2x)^2(1)^5, (2x)^1(1)^6, (2x)^0(1)^7$

6. $128x^7 + 448x^6 + 672x^5 + 560x^4 + 280x^3 + 84x^2 + 14x + 1$ **7.** 792

8. 3003   **9.** 8008

■ **Worksheet 12.6**

1. $2055.00, $113.03, $3168.03;
$3168.03, $174.24, $4342.27;
$4342.27, $238.82, $5581.09;
$5581.09, $306.96, $6888.05;
$6888.05, $378.84, $8266.89;
$8266.89, $454.68, $9721.57;
$9721.57, $534.69, $11,256.26;
$11,256.26, $619.09, $12,875.35;

$12,875.35, $708.14, $14,583.49;
$14,583.49, $802.09, $16,385.58;
$16,385.58, $901.21, $18,286.79;
$18,286.79, $1005.77, $20,292.56;
$20,292.56, $1116.09, $22,408.65;
$22,408.65, $1232.48, $24,641.13;
$24,641.13, $1355.26, $26,996.39;
$26,996.39, $1484.80, $29,481.19

2. $11,481.19

3. $4517.84

■ **Worksheet 13.2**

1.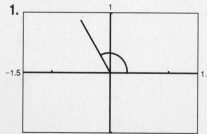

2.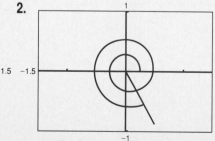

3.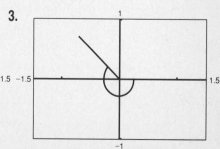

4. 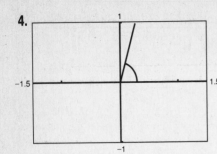 **5.** 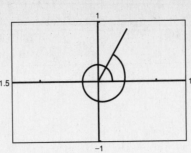 **6.**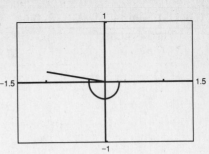

7. $\dfrac{5\pi}{6}$, 150°   **8.** $\dfrac{-7\pi}{4}$, -315°   **9.** $\dfrac{5\pi}{4}$, 225°

■ Worksheet 13.3

1. $\sin 10° \approx 0.17364818$; $\cos 10° \approx 0.98480775$ **2.** $\sin 30° = 0.5$; $\cos 30° \approx 0.8660254$

3. $\sin 45° \approx 0.70710678$; $\cos 45° \approx 0.70710678$ **4.** $\sin 60° \approx 0.8660254$; $\cos 60° = 0.5$

5. $\sin 90° = 1$; $\cos 90° = 0$ **6.** $\sin 120° \approx 0.8660254$; $\cos 120° = $ -0.5

7. $\sin 190° \approx $ -0.1736482; $\cos 190° \approx $ -0.9848078   **8.** $\sin 200° \approx $ -0.3420201; $\cos 200° \approx$
-0.9396926

9. $\sin 245° \approx $ -0.9063078; $\cos 245° \approx $ -0.4226183   **10.** $\sin 246° \approx $ -0.9135455; $\cos 246° \approx$
-0.4067366

11. $\sin 300° \approx $ -0.8660254; $\cos 300° = 0.5$ **12.** $\sin 350° \approx $ -0.1736482; $\cos 350° \approx 0.98480775$

13. Since $\sin\theta = \dfrac{y}{r}$, $\sin\theta$ is positive when y is positive (in Quadrants I and
II) and negative when y is negative (in Quadrants III and IV).

14. Since $\cos\theta = \dfrac{x}{r}$, $\cos\theta$ is positive when x is positive (in Quadrants I and
IV) and negative when x is negative (in Quadrants II and III).

■ Worksheet 14.1

1. 3; π; $\dfrac{1}{\pi}$ **2.** 2; 4π; $\dfrac{1}{4\pi}$ **3.** $\dfrac{5}{2}$; $\dfrac{\pi}{2}$; $\dfrac{2}{\pi}$

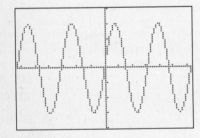   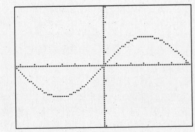   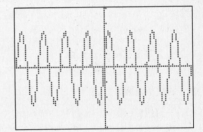

■ Worksheet 14.2

1. $x^2 + (y - 60)^2 = 50^2$ **2.** $a = 50$; $b = \dfrac{\pi}{20}$; $x = 50\sin\left(\dfrac{\pi}{20}t\right)$

3. $50^2 \sin^2\left(\dfrac{\pi}{20}t\right) + (y - 60)^2 = 50^2$ **4.** $y = 60 + 50\cos\left(\dfrac{\pi}{20}t\right)$

5.
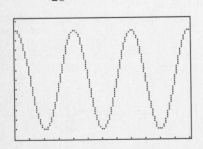

6. The horizontal axis represents time and the
vertical axis represents the height of the car.

7. 60 feet; 10 feet; 60 feet; 110 feet

■ Worksheet 14.3

1. Ellipse, (0, 0)   Circle, (0, 0)   Ellipse, (0, 0)

 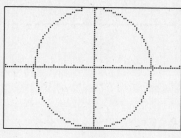 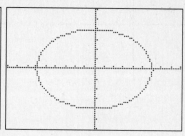

2. Ellipse, (2, 3)   Ellipse, (2, -1)   Hyperbola, (0, 0)

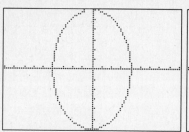 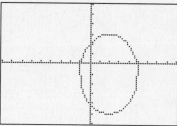 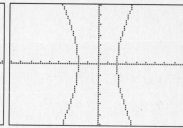

■ Worksheet 15.3

1. 35   **2.** 210   **3.** Exercise 1, because it does not matter in which order you choose the toppings.

4. 120; 120; 1; 1   **5.** 120; 1; 1; 120   **6.** 120; 24; 5; 5   **7.** 120; 2; 10; 60

■ Worksheet 15.4

1. Answers vary.   **2.** Answers vary.   **3.** 1, 12, 66, 220, 495, 792, 924, 792, 495, 220, 66, 12, 1

4. 0.016